D0874446

Mark Twain and His Illustrators

Volume I (1869-1875)

Mark Twain and His Illustrators

Volume I (1869-1875)

by

Beverly R. David

The Whitston Publishing Company
Troy, New York
1986

Contents

Acknowledgments

Every nonfiction work by necessity relies heavily on both the dedication of certain individuals and the accumulation of facts and research data from multiple sources. There are, therefore, many contributors to whom I am indebted. My deep thanks to Professors Russel Nye, who believed in the original concept, and Linda Wagner, who first persuaded me to publish. A special debt of gratitude to Professor Ralph N. Miller who gave me confidence, made patient suggestions, and read manuscript through the many drafts. Thanks also to Professors Phillip Adams and L. ten Harmsel who read through manuscript. My heartfelt appreciation to Professor L. G. Crossman for painstakingly going through manuscript making suggestions and corrections and proofreading the final draft.

I am grateful to Professor Alan Gribben who gave me the heart to continue in the dark days and Professors Thomas Tenney and Louis Budd who provided helpful information. Mr. Larry Massie's lending of rare editions from his special collection is sincerely appreciated.

Both the late Frederick Anderson, former editor of the Mark Twain Papers, and Robert Hirst, the present editor, have assisted me in my research and generously granted me permission to quote from collections in the Mark Twain Papers. The libraries at Vassar, Yale, and New York Public have been most helpful in supplying needed material.

Finally there is the debt to my husband and family who have endured years of a wife and mother with her head full of footnotes; especially John who could not be here to see the book completed.

Foreword

When the Works of Mark Twain series of the University of California Press changed its editorial policy in 1979 and began to include the original first-edition illustrations in combination with scrupulously edited texts, a milestone was reached in the publishing history of Mark Twain's writings.[1] After nearly nine decades during which only the sporadically available Chandler Facsimile series offered an alternative, the public could once again admire the eye-catching pictures that Harper & Brothers casually discarded when that firm took over the contractual rights to Mark Twain's works and started to issue bland uniform-set reprintings, such as the Author's National Edition, to subdue Twain's extravagant subscription-book tendencies.

Beverly David's study dovetails with a recent trend in scholarly editions, and assists in the developing endeavor to call attention to nineteenth-century book illustrators. Her efforts remind us that Twain routinely relied on this visual humor in his travel narratives and novels, and that the typography of his printed text swirled submissively around a multitude of ballooning pictures. Losing this original concept of his pictorially assisted stories has cost us something tangible and crucial in grasping the total effect that Twain and his publishers designed his books to create. Indeed, as Twain became a prominent writer of subscription books, which typically padded their contents with illustrations of every type to facilitate door-to-door canvassing campaigns in villages, farmhouses, and blue-collar urban neighborhoods, he gradually acquired considerable authority (and good sense) in choosing his illustrators and specifying their tasks.[2]

But not all of Twain's interest in graphic arts can be ascribed to the financial advantages of the lucrative subscription-publishing field. He lived in an age in which drawings were thought to be appropriate mainly for reinforcing the texts of "comic" writings; ordinarily the works of Hawthorne, Howells, James, and other "serious" authors appeared in printed forms devoid of illustrations. Thus, Charles Dickens, the Victorian figure most comparable to Mark Twain in terms of trans-Atlantic popularity, benefited from whimsically mannered portraits of Mr. Pickwick, Sam Weller, and Mr. Micawber produced by Hablôt K. Browne ("Phiz") as well as plates by Cruikshank, Stone, Williams, Fildes, and others. John R. Harvey has reminded us that Dickens and his artists "worked for a public which did not easily imagine what it read, and so found illustrations a valuable aid. . . . The common inheritance meant that the imaginations of author and artist could almost fuse in moments of inspiration," and the resulting graphics "could develop a novel's theme subtly, delicately, and powerfully."[3] Michael Steig, too, observes that illustrations in the Victorian novel "have the status of contemporary critical commentary of an especially pertinent kind, since they were created while the novel was in progress and the illustrator in repeated communication with the author. At the very least, we can reasonably assume that such details are consonant with the author's intention." Browne's etchings for *Dombey and Son,* Steig argues, "must be considered an integral part of the novel."[4] Thackeray, of course, was sometimes (as with *Vanity Fair*) his own illustrator, which gave him the ideal opportunity to amplify his written narrative. In fact, one commentator emphasizes that "Thackeray is not Thackeray without the original engravings."[5]

Mark Twain's principal problem was that he could not draw skillfully himself, though he considered himself an art critic (of a lowbrow sort). True, he supplied a ludicrous "Map of Paris" for an 1870 sketch, and contributed several engaging doodles to *A Tramp Abroad* (1880), including a hilarious caricature of a horse and cab "leaving Heilbronn" (chapter 14) and a cock-eyed "Etruscan Tear-jug" (chapter 20), the latter of which has become an icon of free-spending American tourists. Yet Beverly David's book chronicles the many compromises he was obliged to make in relying on the artistic and comedic talents of others—their unreliability in execution, their temperamental vanities, their insobriety of conduct. Nevertheless, aware of how easily a visual rendition could overpower the surrounding printed text, Mark Twain occasionally fussed with facial expressions, physique, posture, positioning, and choice of incident to be illustrated for his sketches, short stories, and novels.

Twain's attention to details about the pictures in his books bore some odd results. That second frontispiece in the first edition of *Huckleberry Finn* (1885), for instance: one can understand why he wished to promote the reputation of the Hartford sculptor Karl Gerhardt, to whom he had become a patron, but the photographed bust of Mark Twain makes a statement quite distinct from putative altruism. The photograph presents a side view of Twain's head, captioned with a gigantic version of his autograph and the explanation, "FROM THE BUST BY KARL GERHARDT." Gerhardt's signature is also legible on the edge of the plaster sculpture at shoulder level. There is much shadow, and Twain's countenance is solemn-looking—a brooding genius with upswept eyebrows, he stares toward eternity in silhouette against a dark backdrop. This striking image was incongruously tipped in between E. W. Kemble's frontispiece sketch of moon-faced, gun-toting, rabbit-clutching Huck Finn and the title page announcing Huck's epistolary narrative. How could the same man who commissioned Kemble's rustic drawing also have arranged for this high-culture form of self-tribute in the front matter, unless he was convinced that *Adventures of Huckleberry Finn* would proclaim his immortality? Electing not to wait for adulation, he congratulated himself in advance with a dignified profile in imitation marble. This bust of a revered author, adjacent to a full-page backwoods sketch and preceding a collection of energetically comic drawings, asks the reader to pause and admire Twain even before beginning the book. Prophetic as it proved, the inclusion of this monument also offers clues to his aspirations and insecurities.

In other cases, Twain's exactitude about humourous illustrations became conspicuous. He was almost as careful in directing his artists as was Lewis Carroll, who dictated to the illustrator of *Alice's Adventures in Wonderland* and *Through the Looking-glass* and even provided some drawings on which the finished versions were based. Twain never went precisely this far, nor could he bring a wry artistic talent like James Thurber's to very many pages of his publications. Perhaps, however, both Thurber and Robert Benchley merely rediscovered the tradition of multimedia productions that had flourished during Twain's long career as an illustrated literary comedian. Benchley's droll caricatures look backwards to Twain's tear-jug and Map of Paris, just as Thurber's little men and plaintive animals seem connected with Twain's efforts to limn a Heilbronn horse and cab.

Essentially the travel works of Mark Twain were illustrated by hand-drawn pictures because the volumes appeared before halftone photoengraving made it commercially possible to reproduce photographs on pages of regular typography; until that process came into use, photographs had to be printed separately from the text.[6]   When it eventually became feasible to include photographs of foreign lands and peoples, Twain eagerly did so, plumping up *Following the Equator* (1897) with scores of on-site photographs. But the true optic achievements in his travel narratives and fiction were the ingenious graphics by Williams, Kemble, Beard, and others, documented in this and succeeding studies to come by Beverly David; the artwork has melded subliminally with our concepts of the adventures, mishaps, and characters described in Twain's writings. And it was probably Twain's continued fascination with the possibilities in the relationship between text and picture that initially attracted him to the biographical labors of Albert Bigelow Paine, whose lavishly embellished *Th. Nast, His Period and His Pictures* appeared in 1904 and ultimately prompted Mark Twain to designate Paine as his official biographer and literary executor. Thus Twain's commitment to the graphic arts colored his interpretation of his responsibilities as a writer, helped account for his mass-market sales, encouraged him to investigate photography as a textual accompaniment, and led him to the biographer who would shape our notions about Mark Twain for generations.

Beverly David's book is the first comprehensive survey of these important functions of the illustrators and their work, and her detailed survey will bring to our attention the potent conjunction of graphic arts, textual design, and narrative content that Twain recognized and exploited. All future commentators on Mark Twain's illustrations and the entire phenomenon of illustrated comic works will gratefully consult her valuable research.

Alan Gribben
University of Texas at Austin
October 1984

Notes

[1] *The Prince and the Pauper,* ed. Victor Fischer and Lin Salamo (Berkeley: University of California Press, 1979) and *A Connecticut Yankee in King Arthur's Court,* ed. Bernard L. Stein and Henry Nash Smith (Berkeley: University of California Press, 1979). The Works of Mark Twain would backslide with another volume, *The Adventures of Tom Sawyer, Tom Sawyer Abroad, Tom Sawyer, Detective,* ed. John C. Gerber, Paul Baender, and Terry Firkins (Berkeley: University of California Press, 1980), which included only a few "selected" illustrations in the rear apparatus; however, the volumes in the paperback Mark Twain Library series by the same editors and publisher would permanently return to an illustrated format.

[2] See Hamlin Hill, "Mark Twain: Audience and Artistry," *American Quarterly,* 15 (Spring 1963), 25-40.

[3] John R. Harvey, *Victorian Novelists and Their Illustrators* (London: Sidgwick & Jackson, 1970), pp. 3-4.

[4] Michael Steig, "Iconography of Sexual Conflict in *Dombey and Son,*" *Dickens Studies Annual,* 1 (1970), 161, 167.

[5] J. Wesley Miller, "Throwing Out Belles Lettres," *American Libraries,* 15 (June 1984), 385.

[6] Among many sources, see Stephen White, "The Photographically Illustrated Book," *A B Bookman's Weekly,* 67 (January 12, 1981), 166, and Warren Chappell, *A Short History of the Printed Word* (New York: Alfred A. Knopf, 1970), p. 194.

Introduction

The large public who read your books have become
accustomed to seeing them characteristically illustrated. A Book with 'Mark Twain's' name attached
to it, without illustrations, would be a disappointment
and materially injure its sale.

Charles W. Webster, 10 August 1887

From the "gorgeous gold frog" stamped into the cover of
The Celebrated Jumping Frog to the peculiar portrait of Aunt
Polly on the final page of *The Adventures of Tom Sawyer*—and
on to the propagandizing illustrations of *The Connecticut
Yankee*—illustration was an integral part of Mark Twain's books
for over three decades. Volume I in this series of *Mark Twain
and His Illustrators* chronologically surveys the years from 1867
to 1875; Volume II will survey the years from 1876 to 1889.
The study explores the influences that illustrators, engravers,
editors, and all the people involved in the complex manufacturing process of subscription books, had on Mark Twain's work.
The study investigates the multi-faceted relationship between the
visual and verbal ideas in Mark Twain's first editions and reveals
how the requirements of subscription publication contributed to
the success, and sometimes failure, of one of our greatest
nineteenth-century American writers.

Mark Twain's first editions, produced for the commercially
oriented subscription market, were a feast for the eyes as well
as a joy to the heart. By definition the subscription book was a
bulky (five to six hundred pages), profusely illustrated (two
hundred and thirty-five prints in *The Innocents Abroad*), crudely
engraved, gilt-embellished and often morocco-bound "parlor-
table" book. These volumes were aggressively peddled throughout the rural countryside by book agents who hawked their
wares by flipping through a prospectus laden with illustrations—
the books themselves seldom printed until after a substantial
number had been subscribed for by customers.

This was the world of the American Publishing Company that Mark Twain entered in 1867 and he quickly became embroiled in the design details for his first subscription book. His first question on whether there should be pictures in *The Innocents Abroad* led to a fast-paced personal involvement: lending photographs from his own collection, fussing schoolmarmishly over whose portraits should be or not be included, roaring with delight when the illustrator captured the author's cynicism on Italian art, and fuming when engravers caused delays that postponed publication dates. But he was pleased with the final product and began again to think about how prints would work in his next book.

With his first success his mind was busy on how to keep the royalties rolling. Not ready with a new subscription-size volume he decided to chance a pamphlet to keep his name before the public. The pamphlet, *(Burlesque) Autobiography,* though financially unsuccessful, proved a training ground for Clemens' future illustrating concepts. In this small book Clemens commissioned a series of "cartoons," unrelated to the text but fascinating in themselves. They formed a visual story of New York corruption, and the political figures in these caricatures would continue to fill the pages of Mark Twain books, both in illustration and story, for many decades.

His next book returned to the usual subscription formula. Slogging through massive manuscript for *Roughing It,* Mark Twain found his chore lightened by his understanding that inserting hundreds of illustrations would help pad his meager narrative. He went into a rage, however, when he discovered that he was being charged for "borrowed" prints—those already engraved for and appearing in other published books. This revelation created a smouldering distrust of his publisher-editor, Elisha Bliss, that would ultimately play a major part in Mark Twain's establishing his own subscription publishing house to produce *Adventures of Huckleberry Finn.*

Meanwhile, Clemens' frustrations about design grew when his idea of fusing the politics of the day with identifiable cartoons by the famous Thomas Nast, ran afoul of schedules and money problems. In the first edition of *The Gilded Age: A Tale of Today,* several less competent artists tried and only partially succeeded in presenting visually a nineteenth-century Watergate. Still, many readers and reporters had a field day matching print and pictures to the national political and personal scandals.

For the next of his now well-remembered books, *The Adventures of Tom Sawyer,* the author left the proven and profitable formula of the subscription book and tried a novel—delightful, though short (two hundred seventy-four pages). The illustrators, if not the author, recreated the typical boyhood of a nineteenth-century Missouri lad. First edition readers sympathized with Tom as he squirmed in his Sunday clothes, wishing himself "naked"—an idea the artists carefully avoided. And the world was introduced to Huckleberry Finn in his "cast-off" clothes, swinging a dead cat by the tail—a vision few twentieth-century readers would ever have. The making of the first edition of *Tom Sawyer* includes a mystery, the still unresolved tale of how of a portrait of B. P. Shillaber's Mrs. Partington became a tail piece depicting Aunt Polly, a plot bizarre enough to tantalize many a future bibliographer.

This study of the illustrations and illustrators of Mark Twain's first editions abounds in backroom drama replete with the tipsy habits of artists, the procrastinations of engravers, the double-sets of accounting books, and the disappointments in the unillustrated English editions. Through this strange arena of subscription publication—a market most genteel writers and readers refused to acknowledge—would shine the genius of Mark Twain and the humanness of Samuel Clemens.

Abbreviations

The following abbreviations and location symbols have been used for citation in this volume.

PREVIOUSLY PUBLISHED TEXTS

BAL II   Jacob Blanck, *Bibliography of American Literature* (New Haven: Yale University Press, 1957), Volume II.

BMT   Merle Johnson, *A Bibliography of the Works of Mark Twain* (New York: Harper and Brothers, 1935).

*CL*1   *Mark Twain's Collected Letters*, Volume 1 (1853-1869), ed. Lin Salamo (Berkeley, Los Angeles, London: University of California Press, forthcoming).

*CL*2   *Mark Twain's Collected Letters*, Volume 2 (1869-1870), ed. Frederick Anderson and Hamlin Hill (Berkeley, Los Angeles, London: University of California Press, forthcoming).

*CL*3   *Mark Twain's Collected Letters*, Volume 3 (1871-1874), ed. Michael B. Frank (Berkeley, Los Angeles, London: University of California Press, forthcoming).

ET&S   *Early Tales & Sketches*, Volume 1 (1851-1864), ed. Edgar Branch and Robert Hirst (Berkeley, Los Angeles, London: University of California Press, 1979).

Hamilton I   Sinclair Hamilton, *Nineteenth Century American Book Illustration*, Volume I (Princeton: Princeton

University Press, 1958).

Hamilton II   Sinclair Hamilton, *Nineteenth Century American Book Illustration*, Supplement (Princeton: Princeton University Press, 1968).

MTB I   Albert Bigelow Paine, *Mark Twain: A Biography*, 3 vols. (New York: Harper and Brothers, 1912).

MTCH   *Mark Twain, The Critical Heritage*, ed. Frederick Anderson (New York: Barnes and Noble, 1971).

MTE   *Mark Twain in Eruption*, ed. Bernard DeVoto (New York: Harper and Brothers, 1940).

MT&EB   Hamlin Hill, *Mark Twain and Elisha Bliss* (Columbia: University of Missouri Press, 1964).

MTinEng   Dennis Welland, *Mark Twain in England* (Atlantic Highlands, NJ: Humanities Press, 1978).

MTHL   *Mark Twain-Howells Letters*, ed. Henry Nash Smith and William M. Gibson (Cambridge: Harvard University Press, 1960).

MTL I   *Mark Twain Letters*, ed. Albert Bigelow Paine (New York: Harper and Brothers, 1917).

MTLP   *Mark Twain's Letters to his Publishers*, ed. Hamlin Hill (Berkeley and Los Angeles: University of California Press, 1967).

MTMF   *Mark Twain to Mrs. Fairbanks*, ed. Dixon Wecter (San Marino, California: Huntington Library, 1949).

N&J1   *Mark Twain's Notebooks & Journals*, Volume I 1855-1873), ed. Frederick Anderson, Michael B. Frank, and Kenneth M. Sanderson (Berkeley, Los Angeles, London: University of California Press, 1975).

N&J2 *Mark Twain's Notebooks & Journals,* Volume II (1877-1883), ed. Frederick Anderson, Lin Salamo, and Bernard L. Stein (Berkeley, Los Angeles, London: University of California Press, 1975).

N&J3 *Mark Twain's Notebooks & Journals,* Volume III (1883-1891), ed. Robert Pack Browning, Michael B. Frank, and Lin Salamo (Berkeley, Los Angeles, London: University of California Press, 1979).

COLLECTIONS IN LIBRARIES

Bancroft The Bancroft Library, University of California, Berkeley.

Berg Henry W. and Albert A. Berg Collection, The New York Public Library, Astor, Lenox and Tilden Foundations.

Doheny Estelle Doheny Collection, The Edward Laurence Doheny Memorial Library, St. John's Seminary, Camarillo, California.

MTP Mark Twain Papers, The Bancroft Library, University of California, Berkeley.

UofM The University of Michigan Library, University of Michigan, Ann Arbor, Michigan.

Vassar Jean Webster McKinney Family Papers, Francis Randolph Rare Book Room, Vassar College Library, Poughkeepsie, New York.

Yale Collection of American Literature, Beinecke Rare Book and Manuscript Library, Yale University, New Haven, Connecticut.

Chapter I

The Innocents Abroad

"Whether it should have pictures in it or not"

In 1867 Mark Twain was a young journalist aboard the *Quaker City*, an excursion liner, hastily jotting down his travel adventures for the *Alta California* at twenty dollars a published letter.[1] In December of that year Samuel Clemens contracted to revise the *Alta* letters for one of the most crassly commercial enterprises in publication, a subscription publishing firm. Although he had been involved in the production side of publishing as a printer's devil, journeyman typesetter, part-time editor, and even amateur illustrator—inserting schoolboy sketches to illustrate early Hannibal *Journal* columns (Figs. 1, 2, & 3)[2]—Twain was naive about book production and publication. His education in that art began in 1868 under the tutelege of a master, Elisha Bliss of the American Publishing Company. Two years later Mark Twain emerged as a wiser and wealthier writer when his first travel book, the profusely illustrated *Innocents Abroad*, became a best seller. The lessons he learned from Bliss, who was as much pitchman as publisher, would influence Twain for the rest of his writing career.

Mark Twain's first book, *The Celebrated Jumping Frog of Calaveras County, and Other Sketches*, had involved him in its manufacture to only a limited extent. The frog story had first appeared without illustrations in the New York *Saturday Press* in November 1865 under the title "Jim Smiley and His Jumping Frog" (no. 119).[3] The instant success of the story brought Twain offers to publish some of his short stories in book form. Among these were a never realized proposal from Bret Harte and another from Charles H. Webb, the latter culminating in the book which included the frog sketch. Twain was apprehensive about the amount of work which would be in the proposed project, but he was enthusiastic about the possible earnings.

Fig. 1. "Local" Resolves to Commit Suicide.

Fig. 2. "Pictur" Department.   Fig. 3. "Pictur" Department.

Commenting on the Harte suggestion, Twain explained in a letter to his family, "I wouldn't do it, only he agrees to take all the trouble. But I want to know whether we are going to make anything out of it."[4]   And, Twain recollected some three decades later, he had had similar feelings about the Webb venture:

> I was charmed and excited by the suggestion and quite
> willing to venture it if some industrious person would
> save me the trouble of gathering the sketches together.
> I was loath to do it myself, for from the beginning of
> my sojourn in this world there was a persistent vacancy
> in me where industry ought to be.[5]

Charles Henry Webb became the industrious spirit who
compensated for the author's expressed indolence. Despite
Twain's remarks, he actively collaborated with Webb in com-
piling and revising material in a cut-and-paste technique while
Webb revised, edited, and otherwise dealt with the tedious details of manufacture.[6] Twain wrote his approval of all of Webb's
decisions in a book-promoting letter for the *Alta California*:

> Webb ("Inigo") has fixed up a volume of my sketches,
> and he and the American News Company will publish it
> on Thursday, the 25th of the present month. He has
> gotten it up in elegant style, and has done everything to
> suit his own taste, which is excellent. I have made no
> suggestions. He calls it "THE CELEBRATED JUMPING
> FROG, AND OTHER SKETCHES, by 'Mark Twain.'
> Edited by C. H. Webb." Its price is $1.50 a copy. It will
> have a truly gorgeous gold frog on the back of it, and that
> frog alone will be worth the money. I don't know but
> what it would be well to publish the frog and leave the
> book out.[7]

Only one other time did Mark Twain give more credit to a book's
design than to its content: in 1889 when he praised Dan Beard's
artistic work for *A Connecticut Yankee*.

The remarks in Twain's *Alta* column must have been based
on communication with Webb rather than a personal inspection
of the book, for some of Mark Twain's facts were garbled. The
editor's name as it appeared on the title page was John Paul—a
pseudonym of Webb's—and the title itself was much longer.
That gorgeous frog appeared not on the back but the front cover
while on the back the frog was blind-stamped (Fig. 4).[8]

Fig. 4. *The Celebrated Jumping Frog* (cover 1867).

Mark Twain's initial delight with the design of the book changed to frustration when he saw the text. Angrily he wrote to Bret Harte: "It [the book] is full of damnable errors of grammar and deadly inconsistencies of spelling in the Frog sketch because I was away and did not read the proofs."[9]   Twain's problems with book design and production began with this work. Throughout the rest of his career he neglected such chores as selecting titles, choosing cover and title-page designs, and making decisions on illustration. He frequently postponed and, at times, actually avoided, proofreading. Painfully, over time, Twain would learn from Bliss and others that these were critical matters. In the door-to-door subscription market, gold-emblazoned covers, flamboyant frontispieces and title pages, and a plethora of inserted and full-page illustrations were as important for sales as appropriate subject matter, a unique style, and correct spelling.

For his first book Mark Twain explained away the unprofitable returns, saying, "As for the Frog book, I don't believe that will ever pay anything worth a cent. I published it simply to advertise myself & not with the hope of making anything out of it."[10] Profit, however, became a prime motivating factor when Twain was queried about publishing a second book.

After the *Quaker City* excursion Clemens returned to Washington and resumed his vocation as a roving reporter and sometime lecturer. In December, however, Elisha Bliss coaxed him into publication again with a very tempting letter:

> We are desirous of obtaining from you a work of some kind, perhaps compiled from your letters from the East, &c., with such interesting additions as may be proper. We are the publishers of A. D. Richardson's works, and flatter ourselves that we can give an author as favorable terms and do as full justice to his productions as any other house in the country. We are perhaps the oldest subscription house in the country, and have never failed to give a book an immense circulation. We sold about 100,000 copies of Richardson's F. D. & E (Field, Dungeon and Escape), and are now printing 41,000 of "Beyond the Mississippi," and large orders ahead. If you have any thought of writing a book, or could be induced to do so, we should be pleased to see you, and will do so. Will you do us the favor to reply at once, at your earliest convenience.[11]

Bliss's mention of the printing of *Beyond the Mississippi* in his first correspondence with Twain would prove ironical since Richardson's book and some of Mark Twain's future books published by Bliss would have interestingly interchangeable engravings.

Opportunely, Mark Twain had already talked to Albert Richardson about subscription publication and was impressed with reports of the financial rewards. When Twain did reply to Bliss he declared that a book could easily be assembled from his *Quaker City* letters. In response to the editor he expressed his concern about the acceptability of his material and the necessity of rewriting. He also asked a curious question about illustrations.

I could weed them [the *Alta* letters] of their chief
faults of construction and inelegancies of expression,
and make a volume that would be more acceptable in
many respects than any I could now write. . . . I could
strike out certain letters, and write new ones where-
with to supply their places. If you think such a book
would suit your purpose, please drop me a line, specifying the size and general style of the volume; *when*
the matter ought to be ready; *whether it should have
pictures in it or not* [italics mine]; and particularly
what your terms with me would be, and what amount of
money I might possibly make out of it. The latter
clause has a degree of importance for me which is
almost beyond my own comprehension. . . . But I know
Richardson, and learned from him, some months ago,
something of an idea of the subscription plan of publishing.[12]

Mark Twain's letter was perceptive in recognizing the problems
involved in revising his California mining-camp humor for an
Eastern audience (a task that would be more extensive than he
realized) although unabashedly innocent in his inquiry about the
book's size and style.

After a further exchange of letters with Bliss in January,
Twain traveled to Hartford to meet with the editor and discuss
plans for publication. On returning, Twain wrote the family
about his new understanding of the format of subscription
editions and his excitement over the verbal contract with Bliss:

The *best* thing that has happened was here. This great
American Publishing Company kept on trying to bargain
with me for a book till I thought I would cut the matter
short by coming up for a *talk*. . . . [I] came up here
and made a splendid contract for a Quaker City
book of 5 or 600 large pages, with illustrations, the
manuscript to be placed in the publishers' hands by the
middle of July. My percentage is to be a fifth more
than they have ever paid any author, except Horace
Greeley. . . . But I had made up my mind to *one* thing
—I wasn't going to touch a book unless there was *money*
in it, and a good deal of it. I told them so. . . . These
publishers get off the most tremendous editions of their

books you can imagine.[13]

Talks with Richardson and Bliss had made Mark Twain fully aware of the potential for profit but only partially aware of the design concepts for the subscription book. Twain would soon understand how much Bliss's "tremendous editions" depended on design.

Since subscription volumes were peddled door-to-door, almost by the pound, bulk was a major concern. The best way to balloon a book to six hundred or more pages was to saturate it with illustrations. These pictures were usually hurriedly drawn and cheaply engraved to keep down costs.[14] Though shabby engravings were profitable, their production often involved eccentric artists, irresponsible engravers, inconsistent quality control, and interminable delays. All of these manufacturing problems surfaced in the publication of Mark Twain's first subscription book—as well as in many of those that followed.

Luckily for Twain, travel books were among the best sellers in the market, and therefore the *Quaker City* letters were exactly right for subscription.[15] The necessary bulk, however, meant that Twain would have to add hundreds of pages of new material even if every other page was illustrated. Early on, Mark Twain remarked about this dilemma to Mrs. Fairbanks, a traveling companion from the ocean voyage and a frequent correspondent. "My book is to make about 600 pages, & I find that my published letters, even copiously illustrated, will only make 250 pages."[16]

Bliss, however, had faith that Twain could produce the needed extra manuscript. Although he was usually as avaricious as any editor and was an acclaimed genius at cutting production costs, he offered his new author a choice of two very lucrative contracts: a flat $10,000, or a five per cent royalty. Clemens, impressed by Richardson's tales of fabulous commissions, gambled on the five per cent.

With the terms set, Clemens spelled out in a letter to Bliss his understanding of their contract. Clemens agreed to the following:

I furnish to the American Publishing Company, through you [Bliss], with MSS sufficient for a volume of 500 to 600 pages, the subject to be the trip of the Quaker City, . . . to be ready about the first of August, . . . I

[Clemens] to give all the usual and necessary attention
in preparing said MSS for the press, and in preparation
of illustrations, [and] in correction of proofs.[17]

As it happened both Clemens and Bliss had difficulty
meeting their contractual commitments. Clemens continued to
be frustrated in trying to compile the mountains of manuscript
needed, and he growled at the later need for lengthy cutting,
revision, and proofreading. Elisha Bliss had his own problems.
His company was involved in the promotion of a number of
books simultaneously: the second edition of *Beyond the
Mississippi,* the first edition of the *Personal History of U. S.
Grant,* and a new volume, Junius Browne's *The Great Metropolis.*
These concerns prevented Bliss from immediately attending to a
new manuscript from a neophyte author. The plates from both
the Browne and the Richardson book, however, would later
prove useful.

Oblivious of Bliss's predicament, Twain completed the
additions to and revisions of his initial draft of the book on 23
June 1868. He then set sail for California to solve an emerging
problem: the *Alta California* had written him about the
possibility of their publishing a cheap paper-back edition of the
Quaker City letters. A publication of this kind would undoubtedly cut sharply into the American Publishing Company's edition. A nervous Clemens persuaded the *Alta* editors not to proceed with their scheme. Breathing more easily, he returned and
immediately contacted Bliss to try to negotiate a prompt date for
issuing his book. The two men could not, however, agree upon a
date. In August Clemens traveled to Hartford to settle at least
the matter of the book's design.[18] By early September he was
still asking Bliss about "the engravings—& in what manner have
you decided to illustrate."[19]

As late as October few important decisions had been made.
By then Clemens realized that the book would have a lengthy
postponement. He explained the complications to Mrs. Fairbanks:

[Bliss and I] have had a long talk about the book, &
concluded that it cannot be illustrated profusely
enough to get it out in December, & therefore we shall
make a spring book of it & issue it the first of March.

The publishers are ready to snatch it out at once, with the usual full-page engravings, but they prefer to have pictures sandwiched in with the text, & [I] do too.[20]

The excuse about the sandwiched cuts was probably a ruse since inserted cuts were normal in Bliss's subscription editions. Clemens' letter makes it clear, however, that some progress had finally begun.

In the meantime, a more pressing problem was brewing among the company's board of directors. Sidney Drake, president of the firm, had suddenly decreed that Mark Twain's material was possibly too humorous (or blasphemous) to carry the trademark of their conservative house. During a frenzied meeting of the board he called for a vote of directors to cancel Twain's contract. Bliss, at that time secretary of the firm's board, countered with a threat to publish the book himself if the men voted cancellation. The directors withdrew all objections.

During these long delays Mark Twain had inadvertently got himself involved in proposing ideas for illustrating his book. In his early correspondence with Bliss, he had informed the publisher that both he and Moses Beach, editor of the New York *Sun* and fellow-traveler on the *Quaker City,* had retained pictures acquired during the trip. Beach and Clemens had purchased numerous tourist cards in each of the cities they had visited and even had *cartes-de-visite* taken of themselves in Constantinople. Another passenger, Colonel Denney, one of several Civil War veterans on the ship, had also compiled an album of pictures with forty-seven of the *Quaker City* pilgrims and ship's officers included. In addition, a Brooklyn photographer, William James, had been hired by Moses Beach to sail with them and take stereopticon slides of the various locations.[21] James had fashioned a dark room in his cabin which allowed slides to be developed overnight and thereby made immediately available to both passengers and crew. After the voyage the photographer had advertised his wares in the New York newspapers, listing as obtainable prints of nearly seventy various sites—from the streets of Horta to the Sphynx.[22]

Clemens suggested that Bliss round up as much of this material as possible and have the illustrators and engravers use as models both the people and locations. The photographs which survive provide insight into one of the techniques used for producing illustrations for *The Innocents Abroad.*

The usual procedure for book illustration in the late nineteenth century was a many-staged, tedious process called "electrotyping." In the first stage an artist created an oversized, original sketch for the approval of author and editor. The subjects for the drawings could be chosen by various persons, including the illustrator, the author, and even at times the editor. For *The Innocents Abroad* everyone made suggestions.

With approval of the original artwork either the illustrator or the engraver transferred a reduced image directly onto a boxwood block. The skill of the engraver was as crucial to the final product as the talent of the illustrator. Even if the artist did his own transfer, it was the engraver who manipulated the short, sharp graver to produce the ultimate image on the wood. Hairline cut by hairline cut the graver's tool followed the lines. One slip and the picture was distorted or the block was ruined.

If the block was to be stereotyped, a process also popular at the time, molds were made from the wood block from a *papier mâché* produced by beating sheets of moistened paper down into the type. If the book was electroplated, molds of the type were taken in wax and the plates were produced by an electrical deposition of copper, the thin shell formed by the copper being backed up by pouring in molten type-metal. These "electros," as they were called, were next mounted on "type high" blocks and inserted into the blank spaces in the standing type of print-page block. The complex process for electros was initially time-consuming and expensive, but it had distinct advantages over the older method of printing directly from wood blocks or from the *papier mâché* method of stereotyping. Copper electros were many times more durable than wood or paper; they would run off many more prints before they deteriorated.[2 3]   Most important to subscription publication, which depended so heavily on illustration, the electros provided a reserve of hundreds of completed plates ready to insert into any print page, in any book, at any time. The ease with which plates could be reused would cause a good deal of friction between Clemens and Bliss in the manufacture of *Roughing It.*

By the late 1860's shortcuts and new materials were being developed to streamline even the electrotyping process. Improved photographic advances now made it possible to project images (the *cartes-de-visites,* stereopticon slides, and tourist cards for Twain's book) directly onto "photosensitive" blocks. The block itself was then developed in the same manner as a photograph. This process, however, was probably used for few (if any) of the many portraits and pictures of exotic locations in *The Innocents Abroad* since Twain talks of a "new photo-process" for the first time a decade later when deliberating about the illustration process for *A Tramp Abroad*.[24]

Pleased at the availability of so much first-hand material, Bliss gathered as many of the pictures as possible and turned over the production of the illustrations themselves to Fay and Cox, a New York-based graphics firm.[25] To create most of the original sketches the company hired True Williams, a well-known illustrator of the day and a man of considerable talent. Despite his artistic reputation, Williams had a habit of going off on alcoholic benders in the middle of his commissions. Fortunately, with only an occasional drinking bout while working on *The Innocents Abroad*, Williams was able to produce most of the drawings, although his initials appear on only four prints.[26]

Other artists seldom mentioned in research done on the first editions of *The Innocents Abroad*, people not connected with Fay and Cox, also contributed to Twain's book. Most significant was Roswell Morse Shurtleff. Shurtleff can be identified as a contributer because he signed four cuts: detailed landscapes of Genoa, Pisa, and Pompeii (Fig. 5). One surmises that many more of the location studies are his, since a number match his particular style.[27] Shurtleff would again serve in a minor illustrating role in *Roughing*

Two other names, Evans and Sargent, also appear on four prints in the first edition. Subscription illustrators, unless celebrated artists, customarily did not bother to sign prints. If they did sign there was no absolute tradition concerning the position for markings—although most of them were placed in the lower right-hand corner of the print. Engravers, however, quick to take offense at being seen in a subordinate position to the other craftsmen, frequently signed their initial or mark in the same corner. Unfortunately it is impossible at this date to identify Evans or Sargent as either illustrators or engravers for the first edition of *The Innocents Abroad*[28] (Figs. 6 & 7).

By February 1869, Bliss had cleared his desk of other company affairs and could turn his attention to Twain's book. While Clemens was in Elmira visiting his intended wife, Olivia Langdon, Bliss wrote with enthusiasm about progress on the book:

FORUM OF JUSTICE.—POMPEII.

Fig. 5. FORUM OF JUSTICE. – POMPEII.

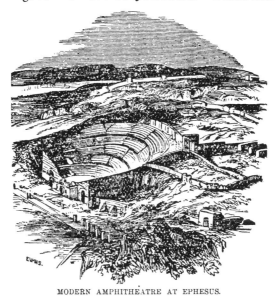

MODERN AMPHITHEATRE AT EPHESUS.

Fig. 6. MODERN AMPHITHEATRE AT EPHESUS.

MOUNT TABOR.

Fig. 7. MOUNT TABOR.

Now about the *Book.* Would say that we have no proofs as yet to send. We are pushing things now very rapidly however. We are about ready to begin to electrotype. We are *filling it with Engravings.* We had an artist from N. York here 2 or 3 weeks reading MS & drawing sketches. They are now in hands of engravers, & we receive *first batch of them* this week when we can push the *electrotyping* rapidly. We think you will be very much pleased with the style in which we are getting it up. We are inserting copy of enclosed in every book we send out & are spreading the report of the Book in all

circulars &c &c. We anticipate a good sale for it—&
think we will *disappoint* you *some* in the result. We
hope *agreeably*. There will be about *200* engravings in
the Book we think. We have 150 now in ready.
We have a lot from Beach & use some of yours also. We
shall hurry the thing up rapidly as soon as we begin to
get engravings, as above. . . . We are spending a good
deal of money on it, more than on any book we ever got
out except perhaps Miss. [*Beyond the Mississippi*],
which this will very much resemble.[29]

This letter is a mine of information on the production of
the illustrations for the book. The New York artist mentioned
by Bliss may well have been Roswell Shurtleff and here Bliss
acknowledges the presence of other illustrators. He also
confirms that the engravers used both Clemens' and Beach's
photographs for some of their designs. Though Bliss obviously
enclosed one of the completed engravings—about which we will
explain more later—and claimed that they were rapidly
progressing, later letters establish that at this time there were
fewer than 150 engravings ready for the electrotypers. The
letter's puzzling reference to a resemblance between *Beyond the
Mississippi* and *The Innocents Abroad* was here merely a general
statement of size and proportion of illustration. Resemblance
would become actual duplication in some prints with the
publication of *Roughing It*.

Mark Twain's initial fascination with and understanding of
the function of illustration in his book were expressed in the
many letters he wrote during the days of reading proof and
making corrections in *The Innocents Abroad*. He replied to Bliss
four days after the editor's February letter, "I am glad of the
pictures—the more we have, the better the book will sell."[30]
And his pleasure increased as he wrote to Olivia Langdon at
about the same time:

"I like the pictures (for the book) ever so much." Only
a dozen or two of them are finished, but they are very
artistically engraved. Some of the little Cathedral
views are very fine. Many of the pictures are simply
illustrative of incidents. They are drawn by a young
artist of considerable talent.[31]

A week later Mark Twain wrote of his appreciation again, this time to Mrs. Fairbanks:

> You ought to see the pictures—they are *very* gay—& they are ingeniously drawn & daintily engraved, too. I have examined proofs of eighty of them, so far, and like them all. I would have sent you some . . . but I only could keep a dozen (cut them out of the pages while reading proof,)—mailed them to Livy at noon.[32]

This was the spring of 1869. Though the book was not ready to be issued at least some of the design problems were settled. Mark Twain's remarks about the illustrations were, at this stage, routine, non-judgmental, and appreciative. His later comments would be more questioning and caustic.

Because Moses Beach had had such a large cache of material from the pilgrim voyage, Williams and other illustrators traveled to New York City to rummage for ideas for their original sketches. The visit was an inspirational and social success since Beach had gone to a good deal of trouble making houseroom for his guests. They, in turn, insisted that Bliss include Beach's portrait in the book (Fig. 8). Apparently Mark Twain had not been consulted, and when he saw the cut he complained to Mrs. Fairbanks: "I was sorry they put Beach in, simply because the letter-press did not seem to call for it." Continuing, he admitted that Beach had been helpful and finally allowed, "it is all right."[33] As it would turn out, many of the portraits in the book had much less reason for being included than Beach's. Some were included at Twain's urging, some just because they were handy, and some because they helped fill empty space. Many would later provide interesting puzzles for future critics and bibliographers.

The Beach, Clemens, and Denney collections—with probably some other passengers' additions—provided scores of portrait images for the engravers to work from. When Clemens examined the likenesses in proof he was again delighted. In another letter to Mrs. Fairbanks he listed some of the people:

> The pictures *are* good, if I do say it myself. There is a multitude of them—among them good portraits of

Dan, Duncan, Beach, Sultan of Turkey, Viceroy of Egypt,
Napoleon (I think,) & a poor picture of Queen of Greece
—& above all, a rear view of Jack & his half-soled
pantaloons. Dan's and Duncan's portraits are *very*
good.[34]

From the beginning Clemens had intended that Dan Slote's picture should be inserted and he had so informed Mrs. Fairbanks:
"We'll have Dan in (copied neatly from his photo)."[35]   Handsome Dan had been the author's friend and sometime cabin-mate
aboard the *Quaker City.* At first meeting Clemens may have mis-
taken Dan for a minister, for he listed him in his journal as "Rev.
Daniel Slote."[36]   Clemens was probably contemplating a lively
conversational, though a temperate trip, since his journal listed
many men of the cloth.   Later, however, he described Dan
and his habits more accurately: "a splendid, immoral, tobacco-
smoking, wine-drinking, godless roommate who is as good and
true and right-minded a man as ever lived"[37] (Figs. 9 & 10).
     Imbibing wine and exhaling tobacco smoke, the two men
had a fine time on their ocean picnic.   They continued to be
friends for many years.   Unfortunately, they later became part-
ners in an engraving company, working on a German Kaolatype
machine for book illustration.   Once linked in commerce, the
two men changed their perception of each other.   Years later
Clemens recalled his friend as "only a pick-pocker [*sic*], more
base than ordinary pick-pockets. . . . I came very near sending
him to the penitentiary."[38]
     The "Duncan" of Clemens' letter was C. C. Duncan, captain
of the *Quaker City.*   In the announcement for the cruise Duncan
had been described as "A Captain . . . who never swore an oath—
never drank a glass of liquor, and though he has crossed the
Atlantic *fifty-eight* times, never suffered a shipwreck."[39]
Though the cruise brochure may have been good public relations,
Clemens had a more factual view of the skipper.   Ten years later,
in a column published in the New York *World,* Clemens would
call the captain the "loudest, the longest, the most irrepressible &
inextinguishable suppliant among the Quaker City's pilgrims."[40]
He further referred to him as merely the "head waiter" of the
Holy Land cruise.[41]
     The *World* remarks were Clemens' response to Duncan's
being accused of misappropriation over the years of the ship's
funds.   Twice Clemens granted interviews denouncing Duncan's

MOSES S. BEACH.

Fig. 8. MOSES S. BEACH.

DAN.

Fig. 9. Daniel Slote.   Fig. 10. DAN.

CAPT. DUNCAN.

Fig. 11. CHARLES DUNCAN.   Fig. 12. CAPT. DUNCAN.

character; twice Duncan sued Clemens. Both suits were settled out of court.[42] The captain's portrait in *The Innocents Abroad* suggests a docile old gentleman rather than a suspected felon (Figs. 11 & 12).

To sketch the foreigners Clemens had met on the pilgrimage, the artists and engravers could also work from available photographs. On most of these Clemens had carefully written the names and a manuscript page number corresponding to the description of the individual in the text. This same identification device was used with the Denney photographs. Nevertheless, Bliss, who was reading proof and working on layout, often had trouble distinguishing one person from another and would write to Clemens for correct information.

In one instance, finding no textual reference to a man Clemens had labeled Abd-el-Kader, Bliss wrote, *"Who the devil is this and where do you mention him. I don't get him somehow."*[43] Mark Twain apologetically responded:

> I suppose I put Ab (Abdel Kader) in by mistake among
> the pictures. I don't mention him anywhere. I simply
> bought his photograph in Constantinople because his

father and mine were about of an age. . . . But if you have got a picture of the old Agitator made, don't waste it—put it in, and call it "Specimen of how the Innocents usually appeared, in the Orient"—or *some*thing, no matter what.[44]

Bliss needed no lessons in economy from Twain. He included the engraved cut but declined Twain's costume-related caption. The portrait was simply labeled EASTERN MONARCH. No text was added to explain his presence to the conscientious reader (Fig. 13).

EASTERN MONARCH.

Fig. 13. EASTERN MONARCH.

Another monarch posed no identification problem but his picture did eventually become a matter of interest to bibliographers. Mark Twain had forgotten to mark the manuscript page number on a photograph of Napoleon III—a small matter since the text refers to him throughout Chapter XIII, the obvious chapter in which to place his picture. His uniformed likeness Bliss appropriately inserted in the chapter on page 126 of the first edition. The last page of this chapter, however, contained only seven lines, leaving too much white space to conform to subscription expectations. Bliss found a simple solution for the second printing of the edition. Since Twain had written about the Emperor throughout the chapter, the editor merely added another cut of the monarch, without his uniform, to fill the empty space (Figs. 14 & 15).

NAPOLEON III.

Fig. 14. NAPOLEON III.   Fig. 15. "Unlisted" TAIL PIECE.

Including this cut as a tail piece in the second state was no trouble; an available electro was merely set into the standing print type of the last page of the first edition/first state and the page was run off. The title page and the "List of Illustrations" could not be as easily corrected. These additions would take time and money to reset. Therefore, even though the second Napoleon brought the number of illustrations to 235, instead of the 234 called for on the title page, the revision was never made in subsequent editions. Similarly, no edition with all illustrations has had a "List of Illustrations" which included or identified the picture on page 129.[45]   Through the years, however, the civilian-attired Napoleon has been a handy point of reference. It distinguishes between the first and subsequent states of the first edition of *The Innocents Abroad*.

Other pictures of prestigious people also drew quizzical notes from Bliss. Writing on the back of one photograph, he asked, "Is this sultan of Turkey? who [sic] you saw with Napoleon?"[46]   Twain answered yes, and made suggestions as to the placement for the picutre: "Sultan of Turkey—belongs with

Napoleon III in the early chapters about Paris. But jam him *any where* you please."[47]   Bliss placed the portrait on the page with the uniformed Napoleon and captioned it Abdul Aziz (Fig. 16).

ABDUL AZIZ.

VICEROY OF EGYPT.

Fig. 16. ABDUL AZIZ.   Fig. 17. VICEROY OF EGYPT.

A similar question was asked about the Viceroy of Egypt. Again Mark Twain identified the person, and the picture was inserted in the book (Fig. 17). Asked about an unknown queen, Twain directed Bliss to "Jam the Queen of Greece in any where. She is the daughter of the Emperor of Russia, and can stand it." In the next sentence he repented, remarking, "*No*—put her in the Grecian chapter—that will be better."[48]   He had already claimed that the portrait of the Queen (Fig. 18) was not a very good likeness.

Bliss did more than just jam the Queen into the correct chapter; he also incorporated her and the civilian Napoleon into another of the American Publishing Company's books: Junius Browne's *The Great Metropolis,* just coming off the presses. In fact, the extra Napoleon and the Greek Queen may have been originally engraved for the Browne book and expediently inserted into the Twain's work to fill space. Such substitution was a normal practice in subscription publication. Bliss later dup-

licated a cut from *The Innocents Abroad* called BEAUTIFUL
STRANGER—a boat, not a woman—in Mark Twain's next major
book, *Roughing It* (Fig. 19). Twain's education in the multi-use
of electros would accelerate after *Roughing It* was published.

QUEEN OF GREECE.   BEAUTIFUL STRANGER.

QUEEN OF GREECE.   BEAUTIFUL STRANGER.
Fig. 18   Fig. 19

Portraits of pilgrims and others, along with cuts of such
famous sights as the Leaning Tower, the Milan Cathedral, and so
on, are sprinkled throughout the first edition. The photographic
portraits and the representational drawings, however, are far out-
numbered by the caricatures in which the illustrators and engravers took an obvious delight.

One young pilgrim was accorded both a portrait and a
caricature. This young man, the "Jack" who, as Clemens noted
in a letter to Mrs. Fairbanks, wore "half-soled pantaloons"—the
seat reinforced with buckskin, if we can believe Mark Twain's
description of him on page 609 of the first edition—was Jack
Van Nostrand. Pictures of him apparently caused some controversy between Twain and his illustrator. Years later Clemens recalled a session he had held with True Williams on the subject.

> I had a character in the first book he illustrated—
> *The Innocents Abroad*. That was a boy seventeen or
> eighteen years old—Jack Van Nostrand—a New York
> boy, who, to my mind, was a very remarkable creature.
> I tried to get Williams to understand that boy, and
> make a picture of Jack that would be worthy of Jack.
>
> Jack was a most singular combination. He was born
> and reared in New York here. He was as delicate in his
> feelings, as clean and pure and refined in his feelings
> . . . as any lovely girl that ever was, but whenever he
> expressed a feeling he did it in Bowery slang, and it
> was a most curious combination—that delicacy of his
> and that apparent coarseness. There was no coarseness
> inside of Jack at all . . . but that quaint, inscrutable
> innocence of his I could not get Williams to put into
> the picture.
>
> Yes, Williams wanted to do it. He said, "I will
> make him as innocent as a virgin." He thought a
> moment, and then said, "I will make him as innocent as
> an unborn virgin," which covered the ground.[49]

Evidently Williams and Twain worked closely in trying to incorporate the nuances of Jack's character into a drawing. The picture to which Twain referred is probably not Jack's portrait, which should not necessarily involve inspiration—only mechanical dexterity *if* it had been done by the photosensitive process. The try at "innocence" was undoubtedly directed to one of the off-hand caricatures Williams did of the lad dressed in his fez and pantaloons. One of these was humorously captioned REAR ELEVATION OF JACK (Figs. 20 & 21). This comical caption, along with other humorous legends scattered throughout the edition, poses interesting questions of authorship—how many of the humorous captions on these illustrations were supplied by Mark Twain, and how many whimsical ideas did the author contribute toward the illustrations themselves? (Figs. 22 & 23).[50]

Half-soled Jack was not the exclusive target of Williams' visual humor. And Mark Twain obviously approved of the comical technique, for he called the artfully rendered sketches his "farfetched imaginary portraits."[51] The barbs in these over-drawn burlesques were most often aimed at four characters from the book: the polysyllabic Andrews, the quizzical "Interrogation

Point," the poetaster Cutter, and Twain himself.

"Andrews" was Dr. Edward Andrews of Albany, New York, nicknamed "The Oracle" by Twain in *The Innocents Abroad.* In

REAR ELEVATION OF JACK.

JACK.

Fig. 20. REAR ELEVATION OF JACK.   Fig. 21. JACK.

A GAS-TLY SUBSTITUTE

A PAIR OF CANONS, 13TH CENTURY.

A GAS-TLY SUBSTITUTE.   A PAIR OF CANONS.
Fig. 22.   Fig. 23.

Twain's *Alta* letters, Andrews had been branded as "an innocent old ass, who doesn't know enough to come in when it rains, but who eats for four, and is vulgar, and smells bad . . . and never uses a one-syllable word when he can 'go two better.' "[52] Mark Twain was less brutal when he described The Oracle in the first edition. But even with the milder language, the words, coupled with the inserted caricature of Andrews as a bespectacled poser, leave little doubt as to Andrews' bemused, obnoxious, and know-it-all personality (Fig. 24).

"INTERROGATION POINT."

THE ORACLE.   "INTERROGATION POINT."

Fig. 24.   Fig. 25.

The composite portrait drawn of the "Interrogation Point," however, remains a visual and verbal enigma. The character was a product of Twain's fertile imagination, salted with traits he found in several people. The description in *The Innocents A-broad*—green, rather foolish, and endlessly curious—can be taken as Twain's assessment of at least three of the young bucks on the cruise: Greer, Van Nostrand, and Charles Langdon. In one letter to Mrs. Fairbanks, Twain seems to have identified him as Frederick Greer.[53] The caricature of the questioning young man in the first edition, however, most resembles a closely shaven Charlie Langdon (Fig. 25). And the lad may have been the unknowing model, the illustrators probably choosing at random from the photographs of young men they had at hand (Fig. 26).[54]

Fig. 26. Charles Langdon.

The caricature of Cutter for the book was the most far-fetched of all, a joke perpetrated *by* Twain or *on* him. Cutter's full name was Bloodgood Haviland Cutter, the fool immortalized by Twain as the Poet Lariat in *The Innocents Abroad.* According to the text he tried the patience of all by reading his doggerel to Consuls, commanders, hotel-keepers,

Arabs, and the Dutch—to anybody who would submit to him.[55]
The picture of this self-styled poet in the first edition, however,
was not Cutter but a good likeness of a frenzied Mark Twain in
the throes of literary creation (Figs. 27 & 28).

"POET LARIAT."

"POET LARIAT."	Mark Twain, 6 October 1867.
Fig. 27.	Fig. 28.

Clemens may not have instigated the visual gag but he heartily approved of it, writing Mrs. Fairbanks: "How do you like the
enclosed portrait of Mr. Cutter which I [snaked] cut it out of
the proofs [Livy and I] have been reading[?] Andrews always
distorted the phrase 'Poet Laureate' into Poet Lariat if you
remember."[56]

Twenty years later when he published his collected verse in
a vanity press edition, Cutter billed himself on the title page as

"Mark Twain's 'Larriat' [sic] in 'Innocents Abroad' "[57]   (Fig. 29). To insure that his readers understood the importance of this connection, Cutter added a picture of himself and a facsimile signature for the frontispiece of his book (Fig. 30). Clemens would probably not have approved of so blatant an exploitation, but there is no extant statement about the publication from either author.

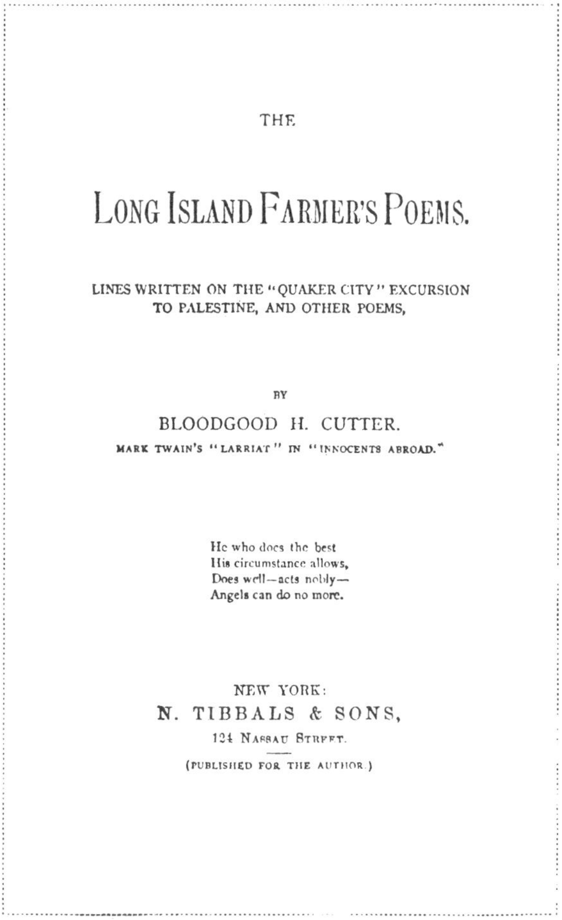

THE

LONG ISLAND FARMER'S POEMS.

LINES WRITTEN ON THE "QUAKER CITY" EXCURSION
TO PALESTINE, AND OTHER POEMS,

BY

BLOODGOOD H. CUTTER.

MARK TWAIN'S "LARRIAT" IN "INNOCENTS ABROAD."

He who does the best
His circumstance allows,
Does well—acts nobly—
Angels can do no more.

NEW YORK:
N. TIBBALS & SONS,
124 NASSAU STREET.

(PUBLISHED FOR THE AUTHOR.)

Fig. 29. LONG ISLAND FARMER'S POEMS.

THE
LONG ISLAND FARMER
POET.

Fig. 30. Bloodgood H. Cutter.

Mark Twain, as the author-narrator-traveler in the book, was, predictably, the most liberally pictured of the characters. Nevertheless, there was no portrait likeness of him. He explained this omission to Olivia Langdon:

> They wanted to make a portrait of me—steel engraving —for a frontispiece; but I naturally objected—refused, rather; that is a sort of impertinent intrusion upon the public that . . . should be left to the patent-medicine gentry.[58]

On the same day (13 March 1869) he wrote to Mrs. Fairbanks:

> They want to put a steel portrait of me in, for a frontispiece, but I refused—I hate the effrontery of shoving the pictures of nobodies under people's noses in that way, after the fashion of quacks & negro minstrels. Told them to make a handsome *wood* engraving of the Quaker City in a storm, instead.[59]

The artists did have a *carte-de-visite* of Clemens (see Fig. 28) taken by Abdullah Freres in Constantinople that they could easily have copied for a frontispiece; therefore it was a conscious choice to use Mark Twain in caricature rather than in portraiture.[60]   And Twain's comments to Olivia were accurate. Since he was not known in the subscription market, a portrait would not likely have boosted sales. More realistically, Frank Bliss, son of Elisha and assistant editor at the publishing firm, put his finger directly on the explanation for so many caricatures: "One of the charms of 'Innocents' pictures was that people could see how *MT* looked in an awkward situation."[61]

Humor was so much a part of the narrative that it was logical to extend the comedy by having the author appear in cartoon form. However, Clemens' repetitious objections to Miss Langdon on using a "portrait" show an intense interest in the idea. He did protest too much, and Clemens would soon desire to join the ranks of the "patent-medicine gentry." *The Innocents Abroad* was one of the few Mark Twain first editions in which the author would choose not to have his portrait prominently displayed as a frontispiece. Interestingly, the *Quaker City* steel engraving, substituted as suggested by Mark Twain, would confuse rather than enlighten the author and future scholars.

One of the first caricatures he saw of himself delighted him so much that he quickly wrote to Olivia, "There is one of me 'on the war-path,' which is *good*."[62]   Elisha Bliss was also pleased with the rendition and capitalized on it by printing it on the advance circulars. Mark Twain loved the promotional idea and thought he might use it. He wrote Bliss's office: "The circular for the Book is nice—it is tip-top—it is handsome. I wish you would send me half a dozen more—& if you have plenty to spare, send a few dozen or a few hundred to my agent, James Redpath, 20 Bromfield street, Boston"[63] (Fig. 31).

Caricatures of Mark Twain, like the war-path print he so admired, formed a consistent thread through the narrative of the first edition. Three dozen or so, give or take a few indistinguishable poses, showed Twain in a variety of absurd situations, from charging/fleeing the Bedouins astride a donkey to being shaved/skinned by a French barber[64] (Figs. 32 & 33). Though the author's features were reasonably consistent—True Williams probably drew most of these caricatures—the most recognizable charactics were the large mustache, the flowing shock of hair, and a well-worn pair of checkered pants.

RETURN IN WAR-PAINT.

CHARGE ON BEDOUINS.

RETURN IN WAR-PAINT.
Fig. 31.

CHARGE ON BEDOUINS.
Fig. 32.

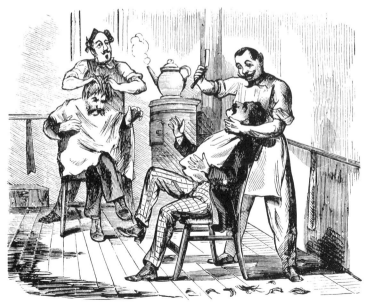

A DECIDED SHAVE.

Fig. 33. A DECIDED SHAVE.

Mark Twain contributed more than his face and physique to the illustrations. For one drawing he aided Bliss in a more direct way. Bliss, busy in Hartford going over sections of manuscript to be illustrated, had come across a Twain passage about an echo the pilgrims had heard while visiting a beautiful Italian Palazza. In recording the experience Mark Twain had written in the manuscript:

> We could not say one, two, three, fast enough, but we could dot our notebooks with our pencil points almost rapidly enough to take down a sort of short-hand report of the result. My page revealed the following account. I could not keep up, but I did as well as I could.[65]

Bliss wrote to Clemens inquiring whether he still had his notebook with the "short-hand" entry, and suggesting that the page might be reproduced as an illustration. The author must have responded in the affirmative for in Chapter XIX are reproduced *two* of the pages from Clemens' notebook (Fig. 34).

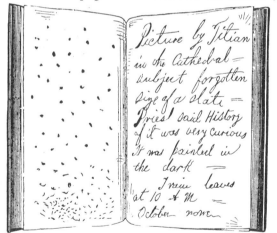

Fig. 34. FIFTY-TWO DISTINCT REPETITIONS.

In the cut, the right-hand page of the open book appears with a text of words that are totally irrelevant to the Echo experience:

Picture by Titian
in the Cathedral—

subject forgotten
size of a slate—
Priest said History
of it was very curious
It was painted in
the dark—
   Train leaves
at 10 A M
October [one unrecoverable word][66]

Though the facsimile is not in Clemens' handwriting, there is reason to believe the entry was copied from Clemens' journal. He had previously used this notebook passage in an earlier *Alta* column, Letter 9, when describing a Titian painting:

> Stowed away among the treasures of the Milan Cathedral they showed us a precious little Titian a foot square —value, 30,000 francs. Brown did not try to conceal his contempt for this thing. He told the priest there was a man in San Francisco who could paint pictures infinitely greater than that—some as much as forty feet long—dash them off in two weeks and sell them for a hundred and fifty dollars.[67]

However, Mark Twain had omitted this entire Titian sequence from *The Innocents Abroad* manuscript and had written no more about the incident. The illustrator, following Bliss's instructions to copy Clemens' notebook, faithfully traced the scribbled notes along with the relevant page of dots which represented the Echo. The page of pencil marks on the left-hand side of the sketched notebook were the short-hand report of the "fifty-two repetitions" made by the most remarkable echo in the world.

When Clemens wrote to Bliss he commented about the possibility of an illustration: "Your idea about the 'Echo' diagram is correct—glad it is to be engraved."[68] There was no statement from either man about the mysterious Titian reference.

Moreover, since using the drawing from Clemens' notebook had been Bliss's idea, he was probably the one who reworded the passage in Mark Twain's narrative instructing the reader to look at an accompanying picture: "My passage revealed the following account."[69]

This small notebook drawing is the only illustration specifically referring a reader to a section of text. At this early date in writing for subscription, making reference to a picture to further expand on an idea was not Mark Twain's usual practice. It would, however, become an increasingly useful tool in the author's future books.

In the captioning for this cut there is another curious inconsistency. The "List of Illustratons" cites the drawing on page 197 of the first edition as NOTE BOOK, while the caption below the picture is FIFTY-TWO DISTINCT REPETITIONS. This oversight was probably more than just a proofreading error on the part of the author or editors. The engraving may not have been finished when the illustration list was compiled and set into type. The compiler, knowing there should be a space allowed for a notebook cut—but knowing only the general content—inserted an unspecific caption for the list. When the cut was finally engraved and set with the correct caption it went directly into the plate and was printed. The list, which had gone into print, would take time to change. Since the inconsistency was minor, it remained as printed. This kind of disjunction between the list and the captioning—along with the irrelevant content in certain drawings and the difficulty of knowing who supplied the captions for some illustrations— remains a help to bibliographers in putting straight the record of Mark Twain's first editions.[70]

A prime example of one of these now unraveled puzzles concerns a strange tail piece for Chapter XLIX. The cut has no obvious relation to the seven lines of text on the page nor to the content of the previous pages. The scenerio for the inclusion of this print—like that of the civilian Napoleon and the tiny Titian—is complicated but does give insight into the peculiar problems involved in illustrating subscription books.

After Mark Twain had completed the original draft of *The Innocents Abroad* in June 1868, he spent many months cutting and revising. Although much of this work was under Bliss's supervision, the editor was not the only person to go over text and request deletions of material. All through the spring of 1869 Clemens' letters to Olivia Langdon testify to his desire to have her carefully go over copy for the book with him: "You'll have to help read some five or six hundred pages. Oh, *I'll* make you useful!"[71] When he went courting he took proofs and engravings along so that they could go over every detail. Later, when the author returned to Hartford, he even tried to get the electrotyper to send Olivia separate packets of illustrations for her approval. This idea hit several snags. Still, Clemens kept reminding her in letters of her duties toward the book.

> What, Livy, think you are presumptuous in advising me
> about expunging infelicities from the book? Not a bit
> of it, darling. I am glad & proud to have you do it.
> And any suggestion you make about *anything* shall be
> honored.[72]

Therefore, it could well have been Olivia who was responsible for the expunging of at least one section of the book —the parable of the Prodigal Son. This was undoubtedly a late deletion since the illustration for the episode must have already been drawn. After the section was cut, the drawing appeared only as a tail piece at the end of the Mount Tabor chapter.

The engraving, innocent enough on the surface, depicts a repugnant ritual Mark Twain had described minutely in the first paragraph of "Home of the Prodigal Son," published in an *Alta* letter:

> As in the days of old, the pensive youth, in curtailed
> shirt and naked shins, still breathes soft nothings in
> the ear of his adored, while she gathers her daily
> camel-dung and sorts it with a critical eye. I know,
> because I have seen the parties at it. Every day you
> see the young ladies of Palestine revelling in masses
> of the refuse of animals with their gentle hands and
> putting the treasure in baskets to be dried and used
> for fuel.[73]

The events leading to the retention of this tail piece can be explained chronologically. Initially both Bliss and Twain had intended to include the Prodigal Son parable in the book. There would be no other reason to go to the expense of having True Williams draw a cut illustrating the scene. During the proofreading sessions in Elmira, however, the genteel Livy had a chance to read the exact nature of the women's work. Olivia, at this time herself the recipient of "soft nothings" in her ear, was repelled at the idea of combining romance and manure. Clemens, in this instance, could be excused for honoring his word, thus allowing Olivia to expunge what she considered to be infelicities. He probably ordered Bliss to take the offending section out. But since the dainty, innocuous cut had been drawn, Bliss used it in much the same way as he had used the cut of Abd-el-Kader—as a filler for an almost empty page at the end of the chapter (Fig. 35).

Fig. 35. TAIL-PIECE—GATHERING FUEL.

As was normal with tail pieces, this picture had no caption printed under it. Its caption did appear, however, in the "List of Illustrations": TAIL-PIECE—GATHERING FUEL. Those words remain as the only clue in the book as to the maiden's occupation. And the caption listing, along with the print itself, testifies to the fact that at one time the story was to have been part of *The Innocents Abroad.*

Of course, Olivia Langdon was not alone in trying to temper some of Mark Twain's material. Two other persons, Emeline Beach and Mrs. Fairbanks, also are known to have pleaded their case for removal of some of the humorous but, to their minds, irreverent passages—and either may have suggested the late deletion of the Prodigal parable. In another instance, however, pleas did not meet with Twain's compliance.

The Italian chapters of the book had given Mark Twain particular problems because he had lost some of his notes containing his account of his travels through Italy, as well as some notes on France and Switzerland. He appealed to many of his *Quaker City* companions to send him their accounts of the trip so that he could have details for his text. Mrs. Fairbanks, Dr. A. R. Jackson, Colonel Denney, J. H. Forester, and Emeline Beach all responded. To Miss Beach, Moses Beach's daughter, Twain had specifically written about his plight with the Old Masters:

> Remember, I am in a great straight [sic], now, & it is hard to have to write about pictures when I don't know anything about them. Hang the whole gang of Old Masters, *I* say! The idea that I have to go to driveling about those dilapidated, antediluvian humbugs at this late day, is exasperating. Why I don't even remember their names—except Titian, Tintoretto, and some of those other infamous Italian Vandals.[74]

Obviously Miss Beach wrote copiously to Mark Twain about the Old Masters, also offering a number of travel tips, for he replied to her, assuring her that he would handle the material with utmost discretion:

> Do I suppose that you are going to tell me about those pictures & go into ecstasies over them, only that I may make fun of them? . . . Put you to all that trouble,— a task which you have done so well, . . . & then make fun . . . of the subject of it? Upon my word & honor I would not do anything of the kind. I have joked about the old masters a good deal in my letters, but nearly all of that will have to come out.[75]

This letter to Miss Beach was written in early 1868. By mid 1869 Mark Twain had become absorbed in creating the mirthfully irreverent passages on the Old Masters and facilely put aside his promises to his young correspondent that he would delete his jokes about the saints.

Beach's daughter was not the most vocal of the critics who wanted the Old Masters treated with delicacy. Conversations and correspondence between Mrs. Fairbanks and Clemens were also filled with reminders from her and responses from him about the responsibilities to and reverence for "fine" art. But like a

mischievous schoolboy, when Mark Twain saw True Williams'
sketches for this section he couldn't wait to send them to Mrs.
Fairbanks with appropriate comments:

> Now you always told me, on board the ship, to revere
> the Old Masters & love them, & speak well of them &
> appreciatively.   It was on that account   that   I   took
> pains all through the book (for I am publishing a book)
> to make mention of them & their works.   And now I
> perceive that my engravers have caught my spirit of
> adulation & are helping me to glorify Titian & those
> other scrubs.   They have made some very beautiful
> studies from the Old Masters—& I enclose the rough
> proofs. (They will be handsome when well printed.) Do
> you know, I think these things unequaled in American
> art. . . . Notice the cheerful satisfaction that is in
> St. Mark's face—& also the easy confidence of his manner.
> Could anything be finer? . . . The St. Matthew is the
> noblest work of art I ever saw.   There is an amount
> of feeling about it that you find nowhere else except
> in the Paul Veronese school.   The pleasant *negligé* of
> the attitude irresistibly suggests Leonardo da Vinchi.
> The [calm thoughtfulness] dreamy spirituality of the
> face arrests the attention of even the most careless ob-
> server. . . . The Jerome is after Tintoretto.   There are
> touches here & there & dainty little effects, that will
> bring that great artist to your mind. . . . Now the tran-
> quil satisfaction with which St. Sebastian goes about
> with a lot of arrows sticking in him, will remind you
> of St. Sebastian by *all* the Old Masters—every one of
> them.[76]

Mark Twain's tongue-in-cheek appreciation here accurately
mirrors his opinion of the Old Masters as written in the first
edition. Forgotten were all the promises to Miss Beach and the
lectures from Mrs. Fairbanks—although he did spare the older
lady, in that he didn't bother to comment on the engraving of
the bottle-nosed St. Unknown (Fig. 40).

Williams' and the engraver's rapport with Mark Twain's in-
tentions throughout this sequence was clearly appreciated by the
author. Twain's satisfaction with the pictures was also reflected
in remarks to Bliss written on the same day he had sent Mrs.

ST. MARK. BY THE OLD MASTERS.

ST. MATTHEW, BY THE OLD MASTERS.

ST. JEROME, BY THE OLD MASTERS.

ST. SEBASTIAN, BY THE OLD MASTERS.

ST. UNKNOWN, BY THE OLD MASTERS.

SAINTS BY THE OLD MASTERS.
Figs. 36, 37, 38, 39 & 40.

Fairbanks the rough sketches: "I think St Mark and the others 'by the Old Masters' are the very funniest pictures I ever saw. I cut them out of the proof to send to Mrs. Fairbanks of Cleveland who always pleaded that the Old Masters might be spared from a blackguarding"[77] (Figs. 36, 37, 38, 39 & 40).

In another letter, this time to Bliss praising the Old Masters, Clemens found an opportunity to gently chide the editor on his choice of a model for one of the other drawings. The cut was supposed to represent the beautiful fountains at Versailles which Mark Twain had described in the book: "Vast fountains whose great bronze effigies discharged rivers of sparkling water into the air and mingled a hundred curving jets together in forms of matchless beauty."[78]   Clemens stated his opinion of the drawing of the fountains to Bliss:

> I *did* "copper" that fountain, but since it looks like the one you got in Paris (Ky.) yourself, I haven't another word to say. You see *I* thought it looked like a lot of niggers and horses adrift in a freshet—but I don't say a word, now, Bliss. I guess it will look well when it is neatly printed.[79]

Bliss admitted his personal substitution for the real statuary but admonished Clemens in a letter: "You get my *idea exactly* of the fountain, when I saw it (but don't tell anyone about that Paris of mine being in KY) some may think I have been Abr-rrod . . . nevertheless, it is good; and will do, particularly the *lamps*"[80] (Fig. 41).

Unfortunately, Williams' drawing of the fountain was poorly engraved and continued to look like something in a freshet, not grand enough to duplicate the French original and not comical enough to make Mark Twain's comments on Versailles a satire.

Mark Twain wanted one scene mentioned in the book depicted with care.   When he still hadn't seen the cut by late spring he sent a letter asking Bliss: "What is become of the beautiful view of Spires (Milan Cathedral)?"[81]   Bliss had to admit that there were still a number of major illustrations unfinished, and in his reply he fretted over the delays: "*The Spire is a full page cut* and not yet done . . . shall have 16 full page cuts . . . Printers slower than the d–l. I wish I was a typesetter . . . . I am sticking in the last chapters now"[82] (Fig. 42).

The time-consuming illustrating process was winding down. Twain, for his part, still hadn't decided on his title. With Bliss pleading for a choice, he finally chose, as he wrote Bliss:

> *"The Innocents Abroad;*
> > or
> *The New Pilgrim's Progress"*
> seems to be the neatest and the easiest understood—
> by farmers and everybody—suppose we adopt it.[83]

With the title adopted the problem of designing the title page still had to be faced. In the same letter finalizing the title, Mark Twain shifted this responsibility to Bliss: "you suggest to the artist an idea for a title-page—you are good at it— remember your idea about it before?—What they *expected* to see —and what they *did* see?"[84]

Bliss made an easy editorial choice. He combined what they did see, the details which had already been drawn by the artist for the cover design, and had the engravers insert this image in a cloud over the dreamy heads of a group of newly drawn pilgrims standing at the rail of their ship. His caption read: THE PILGRIM'S VISION (Figs. 43 & 44).

The end of the production side was in sight and Clemens was overjoyed. He wrote to his family that the publisher had "spent $5,000 on the engravings. It will be a stylish volume";[85] and to Livy he bragged about the two hundred and twenty-four illustrations (though this was in May and not all the cuts were

FOUNTAIN AT VERSAILLES.

Fig. 41. FOUNTAIN AT VERSAILLES.

ROOFS AND SPIRES OF CATHEDRAL AT MILAN.

Fig. 42. ROOFS AND SPIRES OF CATHEDRAL AT MILAN.

THE PILGRIM'S VISION.

ILLUMINATED TITLE-PAGE—THE PILGRIM'S VISION.
Fig. 43.

Fig. 44. Cover, *The Innocents Abroad* or *The New Pilgrim's Progress*, 1869.

done), the need for thirty tons of paper, and the arrangement to have two different printing houses.[86]   By the fourth of June Mark Twain could cheer to both Mrs. Fairbanks and his family: "The last 3 chapters of the book came tonight—we shall read it in the morning and then thank goodness, we are *done*."[87]

Unexpectedly, another snag developed.   Some of the illustrations still had to be completed.   By the twentieth of June the book was almost finished and promotional copies were already arriving at the American Publishing Company from the bindery.[88]   Bliss, however, wanted more promotional time and he tried to sell Clemens on another postponement. Trying to put things in the best light he wrote: "*Unavoidably* we propose to make a fall book of it with every advantage of full preparation and an early start."[89] The rub for Bliss was, the firm was issuing too many books by other authors and had no time available for advance advertising on a new one.

Mark Twain wrote a blistering letter to his editor, correctly or incorrectly blaming the delays on Bliss's preoccupation with other books. Bliss realized that he had tested Twain's patience to the limit. Six days after Twain's complaint, on 28 July 1869, *The Innocents Abroad* was, at last, copyrighted. Bliss explained to Twain his version of the time problem: "The first delay was in order to give us time to *illustrate* it not to give room for *Grant* as that book would be past by the time we could possibly have got out yours."[90] Despite the arguments over the delays, the book was scheduled for issue though Bliss had had to scramble in the last days to complete the edition.

1. The steamship *Quaker City*, the "right stately-looking vessel" which transported the Holy Land Excursion for five and a half months. Although it was thirteen years old, Clemens thought it "sumptuous." [Courtesy Patten Free Library, Bath, Maine]

Fig. 45. Steamship *Quaker City*.

Fig. 46. STEAMSHIP IN A STORM.

In the debate about whether to have a portrait of the author as a frontispiece, Mark Twain had suggested a wood engraving of the *Quaker City* as a suitable substitute. This engraving had not been completed by early June. The illustrators had left and time had run out. Bliss reached conveniently into his pile of available electros for a handy engraving of a ship. What purported to be the *Quaker City* in Mark Twain's first edition was not the pilgrim's ship at all but a full-page engraving of the *Steamer Wright* which had been engraved for a Bliss publication, *Overland through Asia,* and would be reused later in *The American Publisher,* a Bliss in-house journal, as "A STEAMSHIP IN A GALE."[91] Since the "List of Illustrations" had already been set up (using Twain's suggested caption, THE QUAKER CITY IN A STORM) the list was not changed. Bliss, however, knowing that it was not the *Quaker City,* provided a more ambiguous caption below the frontispiece print—STEAMSHIP IN A STORM (Figs. 45 & 46).

At last the book had been issued and was ready for reviews. The most common reviewers for subscription books were the newpapers—very few literary magazines paid attention to subscription market offerings because they considered the books to be of poor quality both in content and design. Most daily newpaper reviews for *The Innocents Abroad* expressed pleasant surprise. They had expected a run-of-the-mill subscription volume, and found instead an exciting potential best seller. Comments on the illustrations in *The Innocents Abroad*— phrases like "handsomely illustrated" or "beautifully illustrated" with a few "excellent woodcuts"—were interlaced with critical comments on the text. One critic went beyond small compliments, arguing that the drawings (which he praised as "humorous without being burlesque") had "caught the infection of drollery from the text."[92]

Surprisingly, some of the more prestigious reviewers joined in. A few writers carped on the volume's enormous size, but even these had praise for the narrative and the drawings. An unsigned review in *Packard's Monthly* stated:

> The book is a ponderous one, containing over 650 pages, splendidly illustrated, and produced in the best style of art by the American Publishing Company, of Hartford. No ordinary 'notice' can do justice to this work. . . . It must be seen (and read) to be appreciated.[93]

Another anonymous critic from the *Nation* grudgingly admitted pleasure:

> He [Mark Twain] has just given us, in a thick book of more than six hundred pages, a record of the tour. It might better have been a thinner book, for there is some dead wood in it, as there has to be in all books which are sold by book-agents and are not to be bought in stores. The rural-district reader likes to see that he has got his money's worth even more than he likes wood-engravings. At least, such is the faith in Hartford; and no man ever saw a book-agent with a small volume in his hand.[94]

It was, of course, the William Dean Howells laudatory review in *The Atlantic Monthly* that gave Mark Twain's book its needed push and prestige—partly just the fact that the book had attracted the attention of so famous a journal and so distinguished a critic. Howells not only praised Twain's style, humor, and originality, he also pointed specifically to the value of the illustrations:

> [T]he artist who has so copiously illustrated the volume has nearly always helped the author in the portraiture of his fellow-passengers, instead of hurting him, which is saying a good deal for an artist; in fact, we may go further and apply the commendation to all the illustrations; and this in spite of the variety of figures in which the same persons are represented, and the artist's tendency to show the characters on mules where the author says they rode horseback.[95]

Howells' appreciation of the care with which Mark Twain, Elisha Bliss, and the team of artists had portrayed the people was nicely balanced with his faintly critical remarks—his sharp eyes catching the flaws of repetition and careless proofreading. Howells' rebuke about the mules concerned a section where Mark Twain, as narrator, described himself traveling to Jericho on "a notoriously slow horse."[96] The illustrations for this section show Twain either standing beside or astride a mule, not a horse (Fig. 47).

Mark Twain eagerly read Howells' review and probably

AN EPIDEMIC.

Fig. 47. AN EPIDEMIC.

smarted a bit over the mule incident. But he was sufficiently in awe of the famous literary authority—and so pleased with the enthusiastic review—that he spent little time worrying about minute inaccuracies in pictures. In fact, he hurried to the *Atlantic* offices to meet Howells, and their long personal and professional relationship began with this visit.

Illustration and design concepts for *The Innocents Abroad* became the benchmark for both author and publisher. This was the book against which each of Mark Twain's succeeding works would be measured. More than forty years after the book was published, A. B. Paine wrote in glowing terms about the teamwork between illustrator and author:

> *The Innocents Abroad* is Mark Twain's greatest book of travel. . . . There is a glow . . . in the tale of that little company. . . . Perhaps [the atmosphere] could be defined in a single word . . . "youth." That the artist, poor True Williams, felt its inspiration is certain. We may believe that Williams was not a great draftsman, but no artist ever caught more perfectly the light and spirit of the author's text. Crude some of the pictures are, no doubt, but they convey the very essence of the

> story; they belong to it, they are a part of it, and they
> ought never to perish. . . . The public, which in the
> long run makes no mistakes, has rendered that verdict.
> The *Innocents* to-day far outsells . . . any other book
> of travel.[97]

No doubt Paine ought to have given some credit to other artists besides True Williams, but his enthusiasm for the collaboration of print and picture in *The Innocents Abroad* was justified. The illustrations, crude and otherwise, did "convey the very essence of the story"—a rare thing in any book, and still more rare in a subscription book. Unfortunately, it would be many years before a similarly exquisite joint effort would work once more for a Mark Twain book.

Twain had taken a gamble on royalties for his first subscription book, and he had won. Author, editor-publisher, and illustrators had proved to be a winning combination. With the publication of *The Innocents Abroad* the author had not only earned financial rewards and critical acclaim but had learned many valuable lessons about the manufacturing process and the business side of publication. The problems associated with subscription illustration—inaccuracy, inconsistency, and frustrating delays—would have to be dealt with in his next major Bliss publication, *Roughing It.*

Notes

[1] Clemens explained to Orion Clemens, his brother, on 8 March 1868, "I only charged them [*Alta*] for 50 letters what (even in) greenbacks would amount to less than two thousand dollars" (*MTB* I: 359-360). Clemens received $1,250 for his steamer fare and an additional $500 for expenses required for land excursions (*Mark Twain's Travels with Mr. Brown,* ed. Franklin Walker and G. Ezra Dane [New York: Alfred A. Knopf, 1940], iii). Hereafter cited as *MTTB.* Clemens wrote 50 letters for the *Alta,* 7 letters for the New York *Tribune* and 3 anonymous dispatches for the New York *Herald.*

[2] When Orion Clemens, editor of the Hannibal *Journal,* was absent from his post, young Sam Clemens took over and wrote two sketches: "'Local' Resolves to Commit Suicide" (16 September 1852) and "'Pictur'

Department" (23 September 1852). To these Sam added woodcuts: "a crude but quite intelligible picture of 'Local,' walking with stick and lantern in hand, cautiously wading into Bear Creek." Local, in this Clemens drawing, has the head of a dog. For the "'Pictur' Department" he embellished the column with two "equally crude portraits of 'Local'" (*ET&S*1, 73). Twain later recalled that he had made the "'villainous cuts' by engraving 'the bottoms of wooden type with a jack-knife'" (*ET&S*1, 73, note 5).

[3] "Jim Smiley and His Jumping Frog" was originally intended for the forthcoming *Artemus Ward: His Travels*. Ward had written Clemens inviting him to contribute to the book. Clemens received the offer late but did write the sketch and mailed it to New York on 18 October 1864. It was too late to be included in the Ward book; therefore Ward's editor, Guy Carleton, sent it to Henry Clapp, editor of the New York *Saturday Press*. There it was published on 18 November 1865 (*CL*1). See also *ET&S* 2, 262-272.

[4] SLC to Jane Clemens and Pamela Moffett, 20 January 1866, *ET&S* 1, 502.

[5] Autobiographical Dictation, typescript made from MT's dictation in MTP, 21 May 1906 (*MTE*, p. 143). Also in *ET&S* 1, 504.

[6] Discussion of Clemens' contributions to the book publication of *The Celebrated Jumping Frog* is in *ET&S* 1, 505-506. "In a private letter to the *Alta*, probably written in early February, Clemens reportedly said that he had compiled a volume of his sketches for publication, but would get some literary friend to look it over before giving it to Carleton, the publisher" ("California Authors," San Francisco *Alta California*, 15 March 1867). Carleton rejected the manuscript and Webb, who was the literary friend Clemens had turned to, later published the book. Carleton and Clemens would remain antagonists for years. Carleton, however, would assume a minor connection with E. W. Kemble's illustrations for *Adventures of Huckleberry Finn*.

[7] SLC to San Francisco *Alta California*, 19 April 1867, *MTTB*, pp. 157-158. "The book was printed by John A. Gray and Green, the New York firm for which Sam Clemens had set type thirteen years before. The blue and gold volume appeared on May 1, 1867; though the author was not entirely pleased with the typography, he doubtless was satisfied with the gold frog that adorned the cover" (*MTTB*, p. 289, note 4).

[8] "On the front is a goldstamped frog. This is usually placed at the lower left corner in a diagonal position with the head pointing to the upper right corner. In some copies the frog is stamped in the center of the cover in a vertical position with the head pointing up" (*BAL*II, 174). "The frog has a peculiar habit of jumping in various positions but it invariably faces the fore-edge" (*BMT*, p. 3).

[9]SLC to Bret Harte, 1 May 1867, *MTL*, I, 124. Also in *N&J*,1, 321, note 30.

[10]*ET&S*, 1, 545-546. In a letter to Bliss, 22 January 1870, Clemens related his prosecution of Webb for copyrights so that he could "break up those plates, and prepare a new vol. of Sketches, but on a different and more 'taking' model" (*MTLP*, p. 30). In early 1870, after the publication of *The Innocents Abroad*, Clemens bought the copyright from Webb and destroyed all the plates he could acquire. "I bought my Jumping Frog from Webb.—gave him what he owed me ($600), and $800 cash, & 300 remaining copies of the book, & also took $128 worth of [fresh] unprinted paper off his hands. I think of a Jumping Frog *pamphlet* (illustrated) for next Christmas—do you want it?" (SLC to EB, 22 December 1870, *CL*2). A year later, 3 January [1871], Clemens wrote Bliss, "I want you to issue Jumping Frog *illustrated*, along with 2 other sketches for the *holidays* next year. I've paid high for the Frog and I want him to get his price back by himself" (*MTLP*, p. 53). Clemens felt that he had lost $2,003.60 by publishing *The Jumping Frog* with Webb (*MTE*, pp. 148-150).

[11]EB to SLC, 21 November 1867, *MTL*, I, 140.

[12]SLC to EB, 2 December 1867, *MTLP*, pp. 12-13.

[13]SLC to Mrs. Jane Clemens and Mrs. Moffett, 24 January 1868, *MTL*, I, 145-146.

[14]Details about the design of subscription books can be found in *MT&EB*, pp. 12-15.

[15]Subject matter in subscription books ran the gamut from biography, history, war, religious tracts, and dictionaries to science and medical self-help journals. Some publications were even mildly pornographic, such as *The Mysteries of Life in the City of Satan.* Pornography, however, was never published by the American Publishing Company. For a list of subscription publications from various sources see *MT&EB*, pp. 183-186.

[16]SLC to Mrs. Fairbanks, 30 January [1868], *MTMF*, p. 17.

[17]SLC to EB, 27 January 1868, *MTLP*, pp. 13-14.

[18]"Clemens was going to deliver the manuscript on July 30 but Bliss asked him to postpone because the firm was just issuing Richardson's *Personal History of U. S. Grant* and would have no time to work on the manuscript. Accordingly, Clemens postponed going to Hartford until the first week in August, & then stayed at Bliss's home on Asylum Street until 18 August 1868" (EB to SLC, 30 July 1868, *CL*1, note 4).

[19]SLC to EB, 3 September 1868, *CL*1.

[20]SLC to Mrs. Fairbanks, 5 October [1868], *MTMF*, p. 40. Clemens had collected some of Mrs. Fairbanks' pictures taken on the voyage.

[21]The Colonel Denney photographs are housed at the Beinecke Library. Some were printed in Robert Hirst, "The Making of *The Innocents*

Abroad: 1867-1872," unpublished dissertation, University of California, Berkeley, 1975 (hereafter cited as Hirst *IA*) and will undoubtedly be reproduced in the California edition of *The Innocents Abroad* when published. I am indebted to Robert Hirst and Leon Dickinson for information on William James. A number of the James photographs have now been found and eight have been published in an article by Robert Hirst and Brandt Rowles, "William E. James's Stereoscopic Views of the *Quaker City* Excursion," *Mark Twain Journal* 22 (Spring 1984), 20-25. A listing of nearly seventy available prints has survived in the *Quaker City* journal of Dr. Benjamin B. Nesbit (copy in MTP courtesy of Leon Dickinson). A number of these photographs were proved in the Hirst-Rowles study to have been used by the artist-engravers for the illustrations in *The Innocents Abroad*. According to Teona Tone Gneiting, "Picture and Text: A Theory of Illustrated Fiction in the Nineteenth Century," unpublished dissertation, University of California, Los Angeles, 1977, p. 97, "109 of the illustrations are wood-block engravings taken from tourist cards or photographs; the remaining 126 illustrations are original sketches."

[22]Robert H. Hirst and Brandt Rowles, "William E. James's Stereoscopic Views of the *Quaker City* Excursion," *Mark Twain Journal* 22 (Spring 1984), 28. The complete list of Dr. Benjamin B. Nesbit's *Quaker City* Journal is in Documents, MTP. A partial list is included in the Hirst-Rowles article. Only a few of Moses Beach's photographs have, to date, been located.

[23]Ronald B. McKerrow, *An Introduction to Bibliography For Literary Students* (London: Oxford University Press, 1927), p. 71.

[24]I am again indebted to Robert Hirst, editor of the Mark Twain Papers, for information on the photosensitive process. Hirst researched the technique described by Paul Fildes in "Phototransfer of Drawing in Wood-Block Engraving," *Printing Historical Society Journal* 5 (1969), 87-97. Hirst states "Fildes suggests fundamentally two criteria for establishing that any given illustration has been produced by photo transfer: (1) an original drawing or photograph is known to have existed, or still exists; (2) a more or less exact reproduction of it printed on paper also exists without alteration in orientation, although frequently smaller than the original drawing. . . . The illustrations in *Innocents* often meet these criteria satisfactorily" (Hirst *IA*, p. 466, note 62). In Hirst *IA*, p. 200, he relates the process to four illustrations in the first edition: Rock of Gibralter, p. 65; Cathedral at Milan, p. 181; Leaning Tower, p. 250; and Far-Away Moses, p. 382. Clemens added to the confusion by using the terms *stereotyped and electrotyped* interchangeably in correspondence (*ET&S1*, 563, note 91). However, a decade later in a letter to Frank Bliss about illustrating processes for *A Tramp Abroad* he wrote, "Of course we can knock down a deal of

that expense, now, by using the new photo-processes" (*MTLP*, p. 114).

[25]*MTB*, I, 366.

[26]Hamilton, I, 244. Signed prints are on pages 103, 132, 150, and 536 in the first edition.

[27]Hamilton, I, 244. Shurtleff's signed prints are on pages 169, 250, 328, and 330 of the first edition.

[28]Hamilton, I, 244. Evans' signed prints are MODERN AMPHITHEATRE AT EPHESUS, page 423 and OAK OF BASHON, page 479; Sargent's signed print is TAIL PIECE, RUINS, page 353. Both signatures appear on MOUNT TABOR, page 521 of the first edition.

[29]EB to SLC, 10 February 1869, MTP. Published in part in *MTLP*, p. 18, note 1. Also published in part in SLC to EB, 14 February 1869, *CL2*, note 1.

[30]SLC to EB, 14 February 1869, *CL2*.

[31]SLC to Olivia Langdon, 6 March 1869, *CL2*. Two days later Clemens sent another note to Livy with an engraving: "P.S. I enclose the Sphynx" (SLC to Olivia Langdon, 8 & 9 March 1869, *CL2*). "This must refer to the full-page illustration captioned 'Pyramids and Sphynx' which appears opposite page 629 of the first edition of *The Innocents Abroad*" (SLC to Olivia Langdon, 8 & 9 March 1869, *CL2*, note 5).

[32]SLC to Mrs. Fairbanks, 13 March [1869], *MTMF*, pp. 83-84.

[33]SLC to Mrs. Fairbanks, *MTMF*, pp. 95-97. Beach's portrait appears on page 615 of the first edition.

[34]SLC to Mrs. Fairbanks, [10 May 1869], *MTMF*, p. 95. In Hirst *IA*, Appendix, Part III, pp. 390-412, is a gallery of forty-seven of the *Quaker City* pilgrims from Colonel Denney's collection excluding Moses Beach but including Slote, Duncan, Cutter, Van Nostrand, and Clemens.

[35]SLC to Mrs. Fairbanks, 13 March [1869], *MTMF*, p. 84. Clemens had appropriated some of Mrs. Fairbanks' photographs: "I have your pictures & I'll distort them & put them in the book" (SLC to Mrs. Fairbanks, 20 February 1869, *CL1*). However, the first edition did not carry a print of Mrs. Fairbanks herself either in portrait or caricature.

[36]*MTMF*, "Introduction," xii, note 3. Reference to Dan, *MTMF*, p. xiii.

[37]*MTB*, I, 322. Also in Milton Meltzer, *Mark Twain Himself* (New York: Thomas Y. Crowell Company, 1960), p. 94. Hereafter cited as *MTHim*. Dan Slote's portrait appears on page 288 of the first edition.

[38]SLC to Mrs. Fairbanks, 21 February 1882, *MTMF*, p. 247. Dan Slote's wife destroyed all the Clemens to Slote correspondence after her husband's death (Dewey Ganzel, *Mark Twain Abroad: The Cruise of the "Quaker City"* [Chicago: University of Chicago Press, 1968], p. 303, note 15). Hereafter cited as Ganzel, *MTA*.

[39]*American Agriculturalist,* 26 (March 1867), 86.   Also in Ganzel, *MTA,* p. 36.

[40]Ganzel, *MTA*, p. 37.

[41]*Twainian,* 4 (July-August 1952), 3.

[42]These and further troubles with Captain Duncan are discussed in *N&J*, III, 18, note 34. Captain Duncan's portrait appears on page 641 of the first edition.

[43]This citation is found in a catalogue: Prospectus of *The Innocents Abroad, American Art Association,* Anderson Galleries, Inc., 1936 [Collection of Irving S. Underhill] Item 72, p. 21, Documents 1869, MTP, "Loosely laid in the volume are the following pieces: . . . A photograph of Abd-Elkader (reproduced on p. 614 of 'The Innocents Abroad') on which Clemens has written in purple ink 'over'; on the verso of the picture he has inscribed 'Abd-el-Kader'. At the foot of the verso of the photograph is the following inscription by Mr. Bliss, one of Clemens' publishers *'Who the devil is this & where do you mention him? I don't get him somehow'."* The reply to Bliss's query is in Clemens' letter, SLC to EB, 29 April 1869, *MTLP*, pp. 21-22.

[44]SLC to EB, 29 April [1869], *MTLP*, pp. 21-22. Kader's portrait appears on page 614 of the first edition.

[45]This "extra" illustration (page 129 of the first edition) was first cited by John Winterich, "Mark Twain," *The Romance of Great Books and Their Authors* (New York: Halcyon House, 1929), p. 585.

[46]Hirst *IA,* p. 467, note 81. According to Hirst this photograph and Alexander II, Emperor of Russia (page 393), Napoleon III (page 126), the Sultan of Turkey (page 126), and the Viceroy of Egypt (page 612) are all part of the Denney collection in the Beinecke Library at Yale. All are small *carte-de-visite* size photographs purchased by Clemens from Abdullah Freres in Constantinople.

[47]Hirst *IA,* p. 467, note 82. According to Hirst, Clemens wrote his answers to Bliss on the back of each *carte-de-visite,* "merely writing 'over' on the face of the picture. In another case Clemens had identified a photograph as 'Viceroy of Egypt & son.' Bliss wrote on the back: 'Is this Viceroy of Egypt?' Clemens again answered *'Yes!'"*

[48]SLC to EB, April Something 1869, *MTLP*, pp. 20-21.

[49]Samuel L. Clemens, *Mark Twain Speaking,* ed. Paul Fatout (Iowa City: University of Iowa Press, 1976), pp. 474-475. REAR ELEVATION OF JACK appears on page 610 of the first edition.

[50]DRIED CONVENT FRUIT (FRUITS in the "List of Illustrations") appears on page 302 of the first edition; A GAS-TLY SUBSTITUTE appears on page 117 of the first edition; and A PAIR OF CANONS, 13th CENTURY (A PAIR OF CANONS OF 13TH CENTURY in "List of Illus-

strations"), appears on page 142 of the first edition. The supposition that
Mark Twain supplied these captions is supported by the fact that years
later he wrote captions for many of the illustrations drawn by E. W. Kemble
for *Adventures of Huckleberry Finn.* See Beverly R. David, "Mark Twain
and the Legends for *Huckleberry Finn,*" *American Literary Realism,* XV
(Autumn 1982), 155-165.

[51]SLC to Mrs. Fairbanks, 13 March [1869], *MTMF*, p. 84.

[52]*Traveling with the Innocents Abroad: Mark Twain's Original Reports
from Europe and the Holy Land,* ed. Daniel Morley McKeithan (Norman,
Oklahoma: University of Oklahoma Press, 1958), p. 23. Hereafter cited as
TIA. The Andrews cut appears on page 70 of the first edition.

[53]SLC to Mrs. Fairbanks, 13 March [1869], *MTMF*, p. 84. In a note
to this letter, editor Dixon Wecter states that it is impossible to precisely
"identify the Interrogation Point, a young, green, rather foolish, and
endlessly curious youth—whose real name Mark gives solely in this letter"
(*MTMF,* p. 84, note 2).

[54]"Charles Langdon may be the 'Interrogation Point' " (SLC to Mrs.
Fairbanks, 13 March [1869], *CL2*, note 3). The cut of "INTERRO-
GATION POINT" appears on page 71 of the first edition.

[55]A description of Bloodgood Cutter is in Ganzel, *MTA*, pp. 41-43.

[56]SLC to Mrs. Fairbanks, 1 April 1869, *MTMF*, pp. 89-90.

[57]John T. Winterich, "The Life & Works of Bloodgood Haviland
Cutter," *Colophon,* Part II (May 30, 1930), n.p. Also in Ganzel, *MTA*, p.
300. In the Documents 1869, MTP, is a sale sheet from the *Alta California*
Bookstore, "Special Bloodgood Cutter List," 1869. One item—no. 12,
"Lines ON THE EGYPTIAN OBELISK"—has, on the title page, MARK
TWAIN'S 'LAURIAT' in 'INNOCENT ABROAD.'"

[58]SLC to Olivia Langdon, 13 March 1869, *CL2*.

[59]*MTMF*, p. 84. Clemens reversed his decision about the portrait just
after *The Innocents Abroad* was published and wrote to Elisha Bliss about
adding a portrait to the remaining issues of the book (SLC to EB, 18 July
1870, Berg Collection). In this letter Clemens remarked that he was now
well enough known. He also asked about putting a steel portrait in
Roughing It. However, Clemens' portrait did no appear in either the late
edition of *The Innocents Abroad* or in *Roughing It.*

[60]There is in the MTP a *carte-de-visite* taken by Abdullah Freres,
Constantinople, similar to the portraits of the other *Quaker City* passengers,
and signed on the back, "Your old friend, Sam L. Clemens Alexandria,
Oct. 6, 1867." It was reprinted as a frontispiece for *MTMF*, ed. Dixon
Wecter.

[61]Frank Bliss to SLC, 27 June 1869, MTP.

[62]SLC to Olivia Langdon, 6 March 1869, *CL2*. The illustration also

appears on page 124 of the first edition, recaptioned RETURN IN WAR-PAINT.

[63]SLC to Bliss, 12 July 1869, *CL2*. Two states of an advertising circular for *The Innocents Abroad* use the illustration of Mark Twain "on the war-path."

[64]Caricatures of Mark Twain appear on pages 34, 36, 67, 74, 91, 95, 99, 115, 124, 132, 135, 136, 148, 163, 196, 248 (back view), 258, 264, 291, 293, 299, 302, 325, 344, 350, 419, 420, 434, 440, 452 (back view), 460(?), 539, 566, 589, 590, facing 601, 627, 633, 639. Even the printing office on board the *Quaker City* had produced an Ichabod Crane likeness of Clemens captioned TWAIN IN FAYAL which was reproduced in *MTL*, I, 130.

[65]Samuel L. Clemens, *The Innocents Abroad, or The New Pilgrim's Progress* (Hartford: American Publishing Company, 1869), p. 197. Hereafter cited as *IA*, 1869.

[66]*IA*, 1869, p. 197.

[67]*TIA*, p. 58. Also discussion of this print in Dewey Ganzel, "Clemens, Mrs. Fairbanks, and *Innocents Abroad*," *Modern Philology*, Vol. LXIII, 2 (November 1965), 136-137, note 51. It is conceivable that Clemens sent his original notebook to the engraver to copy and the engraver failed to return it, for the Italian sections are among those missing in Clemens' journal collections. The notebook cut appears on page 197 of the first edition.

[68]*MTLP*, p. 19. Also discussed in *N&J* I: 37.

[69]*IA*, 1869, p. 197.

[70]A comparison of the legends and the "List of Illustrations" for *The Innocents Abroad* reveals word changes, punctuation errors, and changes relevant to spacing. Listed here are the more important variations in captioning: (1) from "List of Illustrations," (2) actual caption below inserted print.

	No.	Caption	Page
(1)	1	THE QUAKER CITY IN A STORM.	Frontispiece
(2)		STEAMSHIP IN A STORM.	
(1)	26	PAINTING.	96
(2)		POINTING.	
(1)	46	GRAVES OF ABELARD AND HELOISE.	141
(2)		GRAVE OF ABELARD AND HELOISE.	
(1)	68	NOTE BOOK.	197
(2)		FIFTY-TWO DISTINCT REPETITIONS.	

[9]

(1)	77	THE WICKED BROTHER.	listed	216
(2)		WICKED BROTHER.	on	215
(1)	81	"GOOD-BY."		230
(2)		"GOOD-BYE."		
(1)	109	DRIED CONVENT FRUITS.		302
(2)		DRIED CONVENT FRUIT.		
(1)	122	HOUSE, POMPEII.	listed	335
(2)		HOUSE.–POMPEII.	on	334
(1)	133	PALACE AT ATHENS.		356
(2)		PALACE OF GREECE.		
(1)	167	TEMPLE OF THE SUN.		447
(2)		TEMPLE OF THE SUN, BAALBEC.		
(1)	193	"MADONNA-LIKE BEAUTY."		531
(2)		"WHAT MADONNA-LIKE BEAUTY!"		
(1)	206	VIEW OF JERUSALEM (FULL PAGE), FACE PAGE.		574
(2)		VIEW OF JERUSALEM FROM THE NORTH EAST.		
(1)	231	BAD COFFEE.		639
(2)		COFFEE.		

[71] SLC to Olivia Langdon, 12 March 1869, *CL*2. Six days earlier he had written in the same vein: "It will take me several days to get through [old Ms], & in the meantime the proofs will begin to come in. So I shall need you, my little wife. However, most of the proofs will come to me at Elmira, & *then* I can make use of you" (SLC to Olivia Langdon, 6 March 1869, *CL*2).

[72] SLC to Olivia Langdon, 15 May 1869, Postscript, *CL*2.

[73] SLC to *Alta*, 9 February 1868, *TIA*, p. 246. George Brownell was the first to point out some of the facts about this confusing illustration in *The Twainian* 2, No. 7 (1943), 2. The illustration appears on page 524 of the first edition.

[74] Bradford Booth, "Mark Twain's Friendship with Emeline Beach," *American Literature*, XIX (November 1947), 225.

[75] SLC to Emeline Beach, 10 February 1868, *CL*1. Since Miss Beach

had inquired about pictures of Mark Twain, he wrote to her: "I have searched everywhere for my photographs, but cannot find a single one. I must have put them away somewhere very carefully—& when I put anything away, I never can find it again. Still I will institute another search, & will find a picture & send it to you. Those Constantinople pictures were very bad, though. I might almost as well send you a photograph of the Sphynx— it would look as much like me" (SLC to Emeline Beach, 8 January 1868, *CL*1).

[76] SLC to Mrs. Fairbanks, 12 April 1869, *MTMF*, pp. 90-91. The "Old Masters" appear on pages 238 and 239 of the first edition.

[77] SLC to EB, 12 April 1869, *MTLP*, p. 18. Also see *MTMF*, pp. 84-85 for more of this teasing of Mrs. Fairbanks.

[78] *IA*, 1869, p. 153.

[79] SLC to EB, 12 April 1869, *MTLP*, pp. 18-19. "The illustration of the 'fountain at Versailles' [p. 154 of the first edition] was apparently appropriated from an illustration of a fountain in Paris, Kentucky" (*MTLP*, p. 19, note 2). The James photograph of the original fountain at Versailles was apparently too poor a print for the artists to use in their sketches. Bliss later wrote Clemens that the cut looked "like a *whale spout* with Jonah thrown up . . . all *sea sick* & spouting thanks" (EB to SLC, 14 April 1869, *CL*1, note 1).

[80] *MTLP*, p. 19, note 2.

[81] *MTLP*, p. 19. A full-page engraving of "The Spires" appears facing page 172 of the first edition.

[82] *MT&EB*, p. 29. Complete letter, EB to SLC, 14 April 1869, MTP.

[83] *MTLP*, p. 20. The title has, in different areas, curious punctuation changes. On the cover the title has an "air balloon" which serves as the "apostrophe" in Pilgrim's. On the title page the apostrophe, now the usual mark, makes Pilgrims plural (Pilgrims').

[84] *MTLP*, p. 20.

[85] SLC to "Dear Mother," 10 May 1869, *CL*2.

[86] SLC to Olivia Langdon, 14 May 1869, *CL*2.

[87] SLC to "Dear Folks," 4 June 1869, *CL*2. Also, an extension of this letter, "To-day the *last* chapters of the proof came & tomorrow we shall finish reading & be done with the tiresome book forever. . . . It makes just about 650 or 660 pages" (*MTMF*, p. 98).

[88] "On June 20, 1869, 68 cloth, 60 gilt-edged, 250 Leather Library, and 25 half morocco copies of *Innocents Abroad* were delivered to the American Publishing Company from the bindery" (Hamlin Hill, "Mark Twain's Book Sales, 1869-1879," *Bulletin of the New York Public Library*, 65 [June 1961], p. 375).

[89] EB to SLC, 17 July 1869, *MTLP*, p. 24, note 1.

[90]SLC to EB, 14 August 1869, *CL2*. Bliss attributed the delay that did take place in the publication of *The Innocents Abroad* to the time needed for the preparation of illustration and the desire to "take the *flood tide*" of the fall season.

[91]*MT&EB*, p. 194, note 110. Also in Beverly R. David, "Those Pirated Prints," *Mark Twain Journal*, 20 (Winter 1979-80), p. 2.

[92]*Massachusetts Ploughman and New England Journal*, 29 (30 October 1869), 2. Other reviews: Paterson (New Jersey) *Daily Guardian*, 23 August 1869, p. 2; Albany (New York) *Argus*, 13 September 1869, p. 2.

[93]*MTCH*, p. 23. Originally an "Unsigned" review, *Packard's Monthly*, October 1869, ii, 318-19.

[94]*MTCH*, p. 21. Originally an "Unsigned review," *Nation*, 2 September 1869, ix, 194-95.

[95]*MTCH*, p. 28. The original William Dean Howells unsigned review, *Atlantic*, December 1869, xxiv, 764-66.

[96]*IA* (Hartford, 1869), p. 588. The cut, AN EPIDEMIC, appears on page 589 of the first edition.

[97]*MTB*, I, 384.

List of Illustrations: *The Innocents Abroad*

ALL ILLUSTRATIONS FROM FIRST EDITIONS ARE
FROM THE AUTHOR'S PERSONAL COLLECTION.

Chapter II

Mark Twain's (Burlesque) Autobiography

"There are always delays we never calculate on."

In late 1870, Samuel Clemens was still reaping the financial rewards of his first major publication, *The Innocents Abroad,* and savoring a contract for a second subscription book, *Roughing It.* But *Roughing It* was more than a year away from publication. Clemens wanted to capitalize on his newly won fame and, of course, to augment his royalty checks by having another work immediately available for his readers. He therefore proposed to Isaac Sheldon the printing of a small pamphlet. Sheldon was well known to him as editor of the *Galaxy,* a journal for which Mark Twain was currently writing articles, and publisher for Sheldon and Company, a trade book firm.

Mark Twain envisioned this minor book as a compilation of three works: one not-previously-published sketch, "A Burlesque Autobiography"; a slightly revised version of "An Awful—Terrible Medieval Romance," first published in the Buffalo *Express*; and finally a curious series of cartoons for which Twain himself ordered the designs, devised the captions, and established the sequence of insertion. This illustrated portion of the pamphlet, *Mark Twain's (Burlesque) Autobiography and First Romance,* was called "The House That Jack Built." The pamphlet would become an important benchmark in illustration for Twain since it marked his first use of real people as visual targets for political satire in illustration. The idea of prominent figures as models for scathing caricatures, though commercially unsuccessful with this publication, generated a concept of illustration to which the author would return again and again in many of his future best-selling books.

Clemens telegraphed his proposal to Sheldon in early December. A fifteen per cent royalty was agreed upon and Clemens prudently suggested that they time the release of the work for the lucrative Christmas market.[1] Sheldon made an affirmative but cautious reply:

> Your dispatch has been received and we have answered by
> telegraph that we will publish it, and of course do our
> very best as to getting it out in time.[2]

Unfortunately, publication for this, as for most of Mark Twain's
major works over the years, would be delayed by problems with
illustration and design.

Before sending his original proposal to Sheldon, not only
had Mark Twain already written and chosen the sketches to be
included, he had come up with ideas for the cartoons, and had
tentatively selected an artist to do the drawings. These early
design selections are important, for they establish Twain's
responsibility for the illustration. Twain's choice for the
artist was Edward F. Mullen, well known for his humorous work
in *Harper's* and *Vanity Fair.* Since Mullen had also occasionally
worked for Elisha Bliss, it was to Bliss that the author
complained when the artist was unavailable: "I did so want him
[Mullen] for that satire [(*Burlesque*) *Autobiography*] but didn't
know he was sober now, & in hospital."[3] Though talented,
Mullen, like True Williams, had trouble with alcoholism. Mark
Twain was forced to find another artist.

One cannot be sure how Clemens and his publisher chose
their artist; however, one can speculate that they made the
choice after reviewing "political" pamphlets. The nursery rhyme
"The House That Jack Built" had probably been parodied more
than any other, and often with a political twist.[4] Twain himself
had used the tale unillustrated—in a Washington letter to the
Chicago *Republican,* 31 January 1868, when he began a quatrain
of nonsense with "This is the house that Jack built."[5] At a
much later date (when burglars stole the family silver) Mark
Twain issued a warning about "The House that Twain Built,"
using both verse and his own sketch (Fig. 1).

One of the current circulating nursery-rhyme political books
was Whitehead's *The New House That Jack Built,* a patriotic
fable about the horrors of the Civil War. The book featured full-
page drawings facing each page, with captions taken from the old
rhyme. The cartoons had been drawn by H. L. Stephens and G.
C. White.[6] With Mullen unavailable, Stephens, possibly because
of his work on the Whitehead book, was commissioned by Sheldon. Mark Twain may not have been instrumental in the choice,
but it was certainly made with his approval.

Henry Louis Stephens was principally a magazine illustrator,

Fig. 1. The House that Twain Built.

a caricaturist whom critics ranked among the top cartoonists before Thomas Nast dominated the field in the 1860's.[7] Stephen's specialty was political satire, and he was currently on the staffs of such prestigious journals as *Vanity Fair, Mrs. Grundy,* and *Punchinello.* Sheldon and Clemens probably decided to capitalize on both Sheldon's expertise and experience for the illustrations in the pamphlet.

Troubles, however, were brewing. In his original December letter Sheldon had cautioned that it was "of course late in the season to get out a book and there are always delays we can never calculate on, as each step in the process of manufacturing is made."[8] Clemens, having been through some of these delays with *The Innocents Abroad,* decided to intervene personally. He "shot off to New York," staying there seven days while trying to polish his ideas and expedite production.[9]

Stephens, meanwhile, had begun the sketches and, according to another Sheldon letter, the drawings were almost ready for the engraver by 22 December when Stephens' artistic temperament seems to have asserted itself. Sheldon wrote:

> The drawings are to be done to-day & I have engaged Gulick to engrave them. I should have given them to Richardson who is a very good engraver but Stephens insisted that Gulick was *just* the man. They have agreed to make them satisfactory to you. I will send you proofs as soon as they are engraved, which they promise shall be the end of next week.
>
> As soon as the engravings are done I will get the book into type & have you see the whole before it is printed. You will probably see some changes which can be made to advantage.[10]

With Christmas only three days away, and the process completed only to the engraving stage, Sheldon and Clemens realized that they had missed the holiday trade. They decided to push on and issue sometime in January. A series of letters followed through December dealing with the problems in design. On the 29th Sheldon wrote, "The engrav[ings] are promised for the end of this week. It will be next Tuesday before can get them into the stereotyper's hands & begin the plates."[11] Finally, on the last day of the year all the proofs were finished and Sheldon mailed them to Clemens with instructions and comments:

> If they are satisfactory to you please let me know at once. Please also send in "The House that Jack built" just as you want it set up. I understand that you were to make some changes in it to make it fit this case better. Please also indicate where each cut is to go.
>
> I think that these cuts look well but I fear that they are too fine to print as they look here in a [an unintelligible word] *press.*
>
> Please return these proofs & I will send you another set if you desire.
>
> As soon as I hear from you, the whole book will go into type.[12]

New frustrations and delays continued into January. The electrotypers were reluctant to proceed because they wanted to use a particular font of type unavailable at the time. Sheldon was disgruntled because he had received only one sample page instead of half the book as promised—though he finally admitted that, because he had been "upside down moving," he had not supervised the project well. In mid-January, Sheldon wrote that Smith and McDougall, the printers, had prepared eight or ten pages of proof and that he was sending them to Clemens. However, with this he pointed out another problem.

> I think that you will like the page. The dark line about
> the page you of course know does not remain on. The
> borders I think quite neat. The stereotyper has for-
> gotten my (your) direction to have each other page a
> cut. That however can yet be done by simply changing
> the no on the page.[13]

Clemens himself caused additional delay by not returning the proof promptly. In fact, by February he was questioning the issuing of the book, thinking it imprudent to publish humor at a time when Olivia was deathly ill with typhoid. The exchange of letters during all of these months, however, clearly establishes Clemens' connection with the manufacture of his pamphlet. He had early canvassed for an illustrator, worked directly with Sheldon in New York, and was intimately involved in content changes, captioning, and the sequence of insertion for the illustrations.

Stephens took his ideas for the illustrations directly from his work in the Whitehead book, making changes at Sheldon's (and possibly Mark Twain's) direction. Both publications contain twelve drawings: eleven of the cuts and captions in the Whitehead book parallel the same number of cuts and captions in Twain's work and are of the same design (see Figs. 6 & 7). Twain's cartoons, of course, dealt not with the Civil War but with the Erie Railroad Ring and Tammany Hall (topics he had explored before in his newspaper writings) and the author had carefully tailored his captions, as Sheldon suggested, to "fit this case better."[14]

In 1870 the public was fully aware of both the Erie and New York City scandals. Thomas Nast's cartoons in *Harper's Weekly* had publicized the Tweed Ring frauds, though the scale of the thefts was still only partially suspected. And the New York *Times* and *Tribune* had begun to feature editorials chastising both railroad and political tycoons. Today's reader, however, may benefit from a brief commentary on the corruption of the sixties in order to correlate the characters and events in the Twain-Stephens cartoons.

Stephens' first drawing shows a sartorially splendid Democratic donkey with hoof-hand cozily resting on a PLAN for the Erie depot (Fig. 2). Readers contemporary with Mark Twain's pamphlet would have no trouble recognizing A. Oakey Hall as the resplendent donkey—an animal used often in cartoons to represent Mr. Hall, and one which, of course, also suggested the appropriate political party. The caption, "JACK," had its own particular connotation; it suggested a jackass (Figs. 3 & 4).[15] But it was as a dandy, *bonvivant*, jester and poseur that Hall had made his name, a name which drew ridicule from persons suspicious of Tammany Hall politics. Hall had been made mayor of New York City in 1868 and was re-elected in November 1870 by Tweed and Tammany Hall; he was Tweed's tool but there is some doubt concerning his actual power or share in the political plundering.[16] Though he was hardly a leader in the Erie Ring, which depended primarily on the New York State Legislature and courts for its functioning, still Twain must have seen Hall as an instrumental figure in the fleecing of the railroad.

In the second drawing Stephens created a replica of the Erie terminal, also easily recognizable by the nineteenth-century readers (Fig. 5). Inside the terminal, in drawing number three, are piles of smiling money bags—labelled MALT but with coins, not seed, spilling onto the floor—the boodle, no doubt, from the Erie stock dealings (Figs. 6 & 7). The Democratic donkey Oakey, the Erie-Tammany building, and the bags of money set the stage for the story of scandals behind Mark Twain's cartoons.

In the late fifties the bankrupt Erie railroad had been taken over by "Uncle Dan" Drew. He was joined by Jay Gould and "Jubilee Jim" Fisk in the sixties. Fisk, a man of porcine appearance, was an acknowledged genius of finance. With Gould and Drew, he parlayed the Erie into a money-minting machine through manipulation of the railroad's stock.

It was logical, therefore, that the "Rat that ate the Malt" (in drawing number four) should be "Jubilee Jim," resplendent in his gold-braided Admiral's uniform, crouching near the opera house. Mark Twain's readers needed no footnote to remind them that Fisk was a self-styled admiral, or that he had bought the old Pike Opera House and moved the Erie general offices into the upper floors of his now renamed Grand Opera House.

Fig. 2. JACK.

Fig. 3. A. OAKEY HALL.

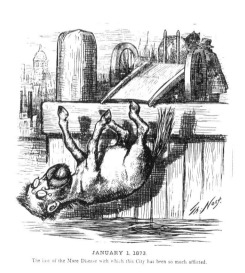

Fig. 4. Thomas Nast, The last of the Mare Disease with which this City has been so much afflicted.

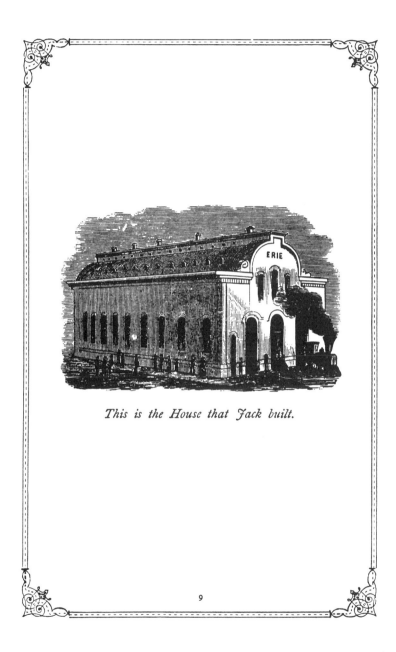

This is the House that Jack built.

Fig. 5. This is the House that Jack built.

12   *THE NEW HOUSE*

THIS IS THE MALT THAT LAY IN THE HOUSE THAT
JACK BUILT.

Fig. 6.   Whitehead, This is the Malt that Lay in the House that
Jack Built.

*This is the Malt that lay in the
House that Jack built.*

Fig. 7. This is the Malt that lay in the House that
Jack Built.

This is the Rat that ate the Malt that lay in the
House that Jack built.

Fig. 8.   This is the Rat that ate the Malt that lay in the House
that Jack Built.

JAMES FISK, Jun.—[Photographed by Brady.]

Fig. 9. JAMES FISK JUN.

Fisk was one of the prime activators in what became known as the "war of the railroads." On the opposing side was Commodore Cornelius Vanderbilt, whose own shady stock dealings had led to his control of the Harlem line (notice that Harlem is misspelled "Harem" on the building in the center of the drawings).[17] Vanderbilt had cast covetous eyes on the Erie and was buying up stock in an attempt to monopolize all railroads coming into New York from the West and thereby to control the tariff rates. To forestall Vanderbilt's scheme, Drew, Fisk, and Gould converted some Erie bonds into stock and sold them—not to Vanderbilt, of course. This maneuver was illegal but not original for the Erie crowd. In his earlier deal to gain control of the Erie, Drew had taken three million dollars in bonds and converted them into stock for sale on Broad Street in 1866. Even after the second dumping to counter Vanderbilt, the three conspirators had in the works a third dumping of five million dollars which would convert into 50,000 shares. These are the figures clearly marked on the bags that have been ripped open by "the Rat that at the Malt" in the cartoon (Figs. 8 & 9).

During the late sixties these stock-watering practices were being chronicled in the New York *Tribune* by editor Horace Greeley, whose editorials vehemently denounced the Erie stock machination. Unfortunately cartoonists in newspapers and magazines often stamped Greeley as a sometime patriot and tarred him with the Tammany Hall brush for his support of Tweed's various urban renewal schemes (Fig. 10).[18]

WHAT I KNOW ABOUT HORACE GREELEY.

Thomas Nast, WHAT I KNOW ABOUT HORACE GREELEY.
Fig. 10.

Be that as it may, Greeley was the cartoonists' delight with his customary white coat, broad-brimmed hat, and baby face framed with an alfalfa crop of whiskers. In the next cartoon, Greeley is drawn as the vigilant cat, "catching" the money-gorging rat, Jim Fisk. It was necessary for Twain to change the nursery rhyme caption from "This is the cat that killed the rat" to "This is the Cat that caught the rat," since "Jubilee Jim" was still very much alive (Fig. 11).

This is the Cat that caught the rat that ate the malt
that lay in the House that Jack built.

Fig. 11. This is the Cat that caught the rat that ate
the malt that lay in the House that Jack built.

Greeley is shown again in the next picture diligently writing his anti-Erie gang columns, with a copy of the *Tribune* stuffed into his back pocket. But in the left-hand corner is drawn "the Dog that 'worried' the cat." This worrying dog wore a collar labelled *Sun*, and had the head of the New York *Sun's* editor, Charles Dana (Fig. 12 & 13). The quotation marks around *worried*, which may or may not have been inserted at Twain's insistence, call special attention to that word, suggesting that the dog in the cartoon is a less successful "worrier" than the dog in the nursery rhyme.

Fig. 12. CHARLES A. DANA.

This is the Dog that "worried" the cat that caught the rat that ate the malt that lay in the House that Jack built.

25

Fig. 13. This is the Dog that "worried" the cat that caught the rat that ate the malt that lay in the House that Jack built.

Greeley had been badgered unmercifully during recent years in Dana's editorials. The *Sun* editor repeatedly asked his *Tribune* counterpart to prove that he was uncontaminated by Tammany Hall. When he turned around and admonished Greeley for not running for public office, Greeley responded with anti-Tammany statements. The arguments between the two editors were a constant commodity in both the *Sun* and *Tribune*. In the cartoon the small size of the dog and his pitifully faint "BOW-WOW" reflect Twain's estimation of the limited powers of Dana and his *Sun.*[19]

Despite Greeley's anti-Erie columns, Vanderbilt's scheme of control was shattered by Fisk's pushing the second batch of stock onto the market. The Commodore tried a new tactic. He obtained an injunction from a State Supreme Court judge restraining the Erie members from converting bonds into salable stock. Judge George G. Barnard, who issued the injunction, was generally known as the tool of Vanderbilt and Tammany Hall. Just before the court hearing, the Erie dumped the third load of shares, flooding Wall Street. An enraged Vanderbilt stormed into Barnard's chambers and demanded that he immediately issue a contempt citation against Drew, Fisk, and Gould for ignoring the injunction. Barnard's court, seen misspelled as BARNAD'S COURT on the horn of the cartoon cow, should have been the patriotic bastion of "The Great Public"—as Twain had noted by his comment below the caption (Fig. 14). But instead of using her one good horn on members of the notorious Erie gang, the "Cow with the crumpled horn" has tossed the worrying reformer, Charles Dana.

Learning that Barnard's contempt order was about to be served, Gould and company made hurried plans. Bundling money, stocks, and papers into trunks, they had the railroad employees move them into the Erie terminal. Drew then fled in a hackney coach to New Jersey with six million Erie dollars. The other two board members, Fisk and Gould, calmly met for dinner at Delmonico's. Surprised by the approach of a constable, the pair sped to the Canal Street docks, where they hired a couple of hands to row them in an open boat to the Jersey shore. The men arrived cold and wet at Taylor's Hotel, thereafter dubbed by the tabloids as "Fort Taylor," where they booked an entire floor of rooms and set up yet another Erie headquarters. These particular capers were not singled out for treatment by Twain or Stephens, but they did provide cartoon material for at least one artist—

This is the Cow with the crumpled horn that tossed the dog that worried the cat that caught the rat that ate the malt that lay in the House that Jack built.

NOTE.—The brand "T G. P.' may possibly refer to The Great Public or The Great People, or something like that.

Fig. 14. This is the Cow with the crumpled horn that tossed the dog that worried the cat that caught the rat that ate the malt that lay in the House that Jack built.

MESSRS. FISK AND GOULD ESCAPING TO NEW JERSEY.—[Sketched by W. Waud.]

MESSRS. FISK AND GOULD ESCAPING TO NEW JERSEY.
Fig. 15.

THE ERIE RAILROAD DIRECTORS' ROOM AT THE TAYLOR HOTEL, JERSEY CITY.
[Sketched by W. Waud.]

THE ERIE RAILROAD DIRECTORS' ROOM AT THE
TAYLOR HOTEL, JERSEY CITY.
Fig. 16.

W. Waud, staff cartoonist for *Harper's Weekly* (Figs. 15 & 16).

Though the gang had successfully evaded the court order, their business efforts were hobbled. The Erie was essentially a New York corporation and they needed access to the city. Gould was the first to realize that the only way to continue business as usual was to shift the railroad war from the court room to the halls of the legislature. With this in mind he shipped trunks of money to Albany, established residence in the Delavan House, and handed out dollars in exchange for votes during the lavish parties in his suite. He was, of course, paying for the passage of a bill that would legalize, *ex post facto,* the sale of convertible bonds. Gould, in the state illegally, was arrested and presented to Judge Barnard's court in New York City. Naturally, Gould was allowed bail, whereupon he rushed back to Albany to hammer home his legislation.

Gould's "donations" pushed the bill through the legislature. It proceeded to the Executive office, where Governor Fenton (hearsay has it that he received a handsome reward) signed the bill into law.

The Albany bill had other ramifications. It not only allowed bond conversion but also prevented interlocking directorates. Commodore Vanderbilt's dream of cornering the eastern railroad market was doomed. Yet he continued to hold a trump card: the injunction and contempt citation were still in effect in New York. Both Gould and Vanderbilt decided to compromise on their positions. Gould would give the Commodore one million dollars from the Erie coffers, allow him to sell his Erie stock on the street without a loss, and give him two seats on the Erie board. The Commodore in turn dropped all formal charges and agreed to lend legal support to Erie business ventures.

Administrative control of the Erie was all but secure. However, Gould also wanted to tie the package tight—he wanted control of the stockholders. Since a large number of the shareholders were English, Gould merely changed the by-laws to prevent shareholders from voting unless they attended the meetings in person. Gould then further solidified his position by enlisting the help of William Marcy Tweed. He had Tweed persuade the notorious Judge Barnard to issue a series of injunctions that countered all moves of foreign investors in Erie. Barnard's court, which had previously opposed the Erie, now ruled in favor of it. The correctly spelled BARNARD'S RANCH sign on the barn door in the next cartoon tells the tale (Figs. 17 & 18).

This is the Maiden all forlorn that milked the cow with the crumpled horn that tossed the dog that worried the cat that caught the rat that ate the malt that lay in the House that Jack built.

35

Fig. 17.   This is the Maiden all forlorn that milked the cow with the crumpled horn that tossed the dog that worried the cat that caught the rat that ate the malt that lay in the House that Jack built.

Fig. 18. JUDGE GEORGE BARNARD.

BARNARD'S RANCH

Stock "Watered" here diligently
watched and cared for
Special protection afforded
against troublesome neighbors'
JOHN BULLS[20]

In essence, "the Maiden all forlorn," Judge Barnard, was shown milking the PUBLIC HONOR and affording special protection for the Erie against the troublesome English neighbors, the JOHN BULLS.

Once the deal with the Commodore was struck, Gould, Fisk, and a soon-to-be-replaced Drew were nominated and approved as the Executive Committee of the Erie. They were instantly baptized by the newspapers as "The Triumvirate"[21] (Fig. 19). In payment (as agreed) one seat on the board went to Peter "Brains" Sweeney, the political organizer of Tammany Hall, who is seen smirking behind the multi-headed Erie Directorate next to the Commodore (Figs. 20, 21, & 22).

This is the Man all "tattered and torn" that loved the maiden all forlorn that milked the cow with the crumpled horn that tossed the dog that worried the cat that caught the rat that ate the malt that lay in the House that Jack built.

39

Fig. 19.   This is the Man all "tattered and torn" that loved the maiden all forlorn that milked the cow with the crumpled horn that tossed the dog that worried the cat that caught the rat that ate the malt that lay in the House that Jack built.

Fig. 20. DANIEL DREW.

Fig. 21. PETER "BRAINS" SWEENEY.

Fig. 22. CORNELIUS VANDERBILT.

The Erie-Tammany combination was now officially joined. The next cartoon depicts a wedding in which "The Triumvirate," Gould, Fisk, and Drew, pose as the groom. John "Toots" Hoffman (now Governor of New York, having defeated Fenton with Tweed's help) poses as the shy Tammany bride. The ceremony is presided over by a priest—none other than "Boss" Tweed!— whose gown features the embroidered slogans "With this Ring I Thee Wed" and "Thee Endow," while the ring itself is engraved ERIE (Figs. 23, 24, 25, & 26). By this time Tweed had also been granted a seat on the board.

Mark Twain had to substitute a "(not)" for the "all" to the nursery rhyme caption of the "Priest shaven and shorn," since he couldn't risk having readers fail to recognize Tweed without his beard. Observing the nuptials, under the outstretched arms of Tweed, are the "best men"—"Brains" Sweeney and his parallel in the partnership, Commodore Vanderbilt. With this marriage of money and political power, the corruption of the state of New York was about to spill over into the rest of the nation.

This is the Priest (not) shaven and shorn, that married the man all tattered and torn unto the maiden all forlorn that milked the cow with the crumpled horn that tossed the dog that worried the cat that caught the rat that ate the malt that lay in the House that Jack built.

43

Fig. 23. This is the Priest (not) shaven and shorn, that married the man all tattered and torn unto the maiden all forlorn that milked the cow with the crumpled horn that tossed the dog that worried the cat that caught the rat that ate the malt that lay in the House that Jack built.

Fig. 24. HON. WILLIAM M. TWEED.

Fig. 25. THE POWER BEHIND THE THRONE.

Fig. 26. JAY GOULD.

The last cartoon in the book finds a strutting cock, "Toots" Hoffman, crowing his message of triumph from his gubernatorial throne appropriately emblazoned with "Excelsior," the Latin motto on the New York State seal (Fig. 27). Hoffman, under the Tweed and Erie banners, was being touted and groomed for the Presidency in 1872. Governor "Toots" is shown delivering the eulogy, "Perpetual Board of Directors. Whoop de Doodle Doo," for the encoffined Erie, since the Gould-Tweed union was fast bleeding the railroad of its assets (Fig. 28).

In a preface to the English edition of *The Gilded Age,* Mark Twain wrote an epilogue revealing the fate of two of the members featured in his *(Burlesque) Autobiography.*

> Our improvement has already begun. Mr. Tweed (whom Great Britian furnished to us), after laughing at our laws and courts for a good while, has at last been sentenced to thirteen years' imprisonment with hard labour. It is simply bliss to think of it. It will be at least two years before any governor will dare to pardon him out, too. A great New York judge [George Barnard] who continued a vile, a shameless career, season after season, defying the legislature and sneering at the newspapers, was brought low at last, stripped of his dignities, and by public sentence debarred from ever again holding any office of honour or profit in the State.[22]

As for the rest, with Oakey Hall no longer mayor, Tammany Hall would crumble, mainly through the efforts of Thomas Nast's cartoons and the New York papers. Horace Greeley, after losing his bid for the 1872 Presidency, would die in a private mental institution. "Jubilee Jim" Fisk would be fatally shot by the new lover of his long-time mistress, Josie Mansfield. And Jay Gould would be forced out of the Erie—though he subsequently went on to bigger and better stock successes and would be featured as a cartoon figure in another Mark Twain book.

But all of this was still in the future. Twain's pamphlet was copyrighted on February 18th and officially issued on March 4th. The series of cartoons in the pamphlet made it a curious pastiche of two poorly written and unrelated stories and a set of completely irrelevant pictures—irrelevant at least to either of the included stories. Clemens had not helped matters by

This is the Cock that crowed in the morn to wake (into existence) the man all tattered and torn that married the maiden all forlorn that milked the cow with the crumpled horn that tossed the dog that worried the cat that caught the rat that ate the malt that lay in the House that Jack built.

47

Fig. 27. This is the Cock that crowed in the morn to wake (into existence) the man all tattered and torn that married the maiden all forlorn that milked the cow with the crumpled horn that tossed the dog that worried the cat that caught the rat that ate the malt that lay in the House that Jack built.

HON. JOHN T. HOFFMAN, MAYOR-ELECT OF NEW YORK
CITY.
Fig. 28.

stipulating that the cartoons should be spaced to appear on every
second page. (In actual fact, there were not enough cartoons to
fill every second page, and so the publisher sprinkled them between page 5 and page 47.) Had the eleven cartoons dealing with
the Erie and Tammany Hall scandals been given a section of their
own, their impact would have been far greater and the pamphlet
as a whole would have been a good deal less puzzling to readers—
then and now.

Reviews of the pamphlet were scarce, and mostly negative.
In some of these, the cartoons came in for more praise than the
rest of the book. The New York *Tribune,* for example, paid a
tongue-in-cheek compliment to the "artistic reproductions of the
pre-Raphaelite school [which] adorn the pages of the work
illustrating the triumphs of modern finance in New-York."[23]
The Boston *Transcript* reviewer, after noting that the book was
"crammed with fun," made specific allusions to the illustrations
rather than to the writing in the pamphlet: "The hits with pen
and pencil will be enjoyed by all interested in Erie and other
Fiskal operations."[24]   Mark Twain's cartoon messages, at least,
were obviously understood.

The Boston *Literary World* was less charitable, having cost-
ed out the production figures to show that the pamphlet was
merely a crass money-making venture by Mark Twain and his
publisher:

The prime difficulty that meets the critic is one of clas-
sification: he feels like a naturalist gazing upon Barnum's
"What Is It?" Is it "fish, flesh, fowl, or good red her-
ring?" The stereotype-plates and illustrations of the
Autobiography cost not far from $400, and for the text—
which would be dear at two and three pence—allow one
hundred dollars. Here we have $500 as the cost of the
book all ready to be printed. The cost of manufacturing
each copy—paper, press-work, etc.—could not exceed
four cents. The publishers announce that they have
sould 40,000 copies. The actual cost of these, including
the making of plates, etc., was $2,000; the cost to the
public was $16,000, the books selling at forty cents per
copy (in cloth at seventy-five cents). This is a living
profit.[25]

Though some profit was made for both Sheldon and Clemens, Sheldon seemed somewhat contrite months later when he
wrote Clemens about another proposed work, stating, "We had
better give the public enough for the money next time. I like to
have everyone satisfied."[26] And a few years later Clemens expressed his own embarrassment about the book, acknowledging
that the quality of the writing was inferior and the satire of the
cartoons pedestrian. He later ordered all available plates bought
up and destroyed.[27]

Despite the essential failure of the experiment—the skimpi-
ness of the pamphlet, the confusing relationship between text
and pictures, and the missed holiday market—major interesting
design ideas originated with this small series of cartoons. Two
years later Mark Twain collaborated with Charles Dudley Warner
in writing *The Gilded Age,* a more substantial attempt at political
muckraking. For this book he wanted Thomas Nast, but had to
settle again for Henry L. Stephens, who combined his talents
with those of another prominent caricaturist, Augustus Hoppin.
These two artists provided many accurate portrayals of corrupt
politicians, though the scene would shift from New York to
Washington.

Notes

[1] SLC to I. A. Sheldon, 8 December 1870, *ET&S*, 1, 561, 562. Telegram not extant.
[2] Sheldon to SLC, 9 December 1870, MTP. Part of letter in *ET&S*, 1, 562.
[3] SLC to EB, 22 December 1870, *CL2*. E. F. Mullen's illustrations appeared in a number of humorous works which would have come to Clemens' attention, including *Artemus Ward: His Travels*. In this same letter Clemens also indicated that he wanted Mullen to do the work on an early volume of *Mark Twain Sketches* (1870-71), reminding Bliss, "You better go to canvassing for the vol. of sketches *now*, hadn't you? You must illustrate it—& mind you, the man to do the choicest of the pictures is Mullin [sic]" (*ET&S*, 1, 572-573).
[4] Iona and Peter Opie, *The Oxford Dictionary of Nursery Rhymes* (Oxford: Clarendon Press, 1951), p. 231. I am indebted to Louis J. Budd for the information on the many versions of the nursery rhyme.
[5] A year later Mark Twain did publish his ironical version of "The Revised Catechism," and at least one scholar credits Nast's cartoons with Twain's inspiration for the catechism (Arthur L. Vogelback, "Mark Twain and the Tammany Ring," PMLA [March 1955], 71). Twain composed and sketched this version of "The House that Twain Built" to state his personal complaints against a trust company in 1908 (DV376, MTP).
[6] L. Whitehead, Sr., *The New House That Jack Built*, New York: Beadle and Company, 1865.
[7] Hamilton, I, 136.
[8] Sheldon & Co., to SLC, 9 December 1870, MTP. Published in part in *ET&S*, 1, 562.
[9] SLC to Mrs. Fairbanks, 17 [December 1870]. "I shot off to New York to issue a pamphlet, & staid over 7 days" (*MTMF*, p. 142).
[10] Sheldon & Co., to SLC, 22 December 1870, MTP. Published in part in *ET&S*, 1, 562-563 and note 88.
[11] Sheldon & Co., to SLC, 29 December 1870, MTP. Published in part in *ET&S*, 1, 563. "*BA1* [*(Burlesque) Autobiography)*] is not in fact stereotyped; it was electrotyped by Smith and McDougall, 82 Beekman Street, New York City. Sheldon and Mark Twain used the two terms interchangeably" (*ET&S*, 1, 563, note 91).

[12]Sheldon to SLC, 31 December 1870, MTP. Published in part in *ET&S*, 1, 563.

[13]Sheldon to SLC, 19 January 1871, MTP. Published in part in *ET&S*, 1, 564.

[14]Whitehead's book has one cut duplicated, the cupola of the capital, while Clemens' pamphlet has one extra cut, a hangman's gibbet captioned OUR FAMILY TREE, p. 6. "Mark Twain adapted this nursery rhyme to ridicule the principals in the Erie Railroad scandal: he must therefore have made some plan for the illustrator to follow" (*ET&S*, 1, 561, note 85). A comprehensive study of the publishing of Mark Twain's *(Burlesque) Autobiography and First Romance*, New York: Sheldon and Co., 1871, is included in *ET&S*, 1, 561-571. The content of the cartoons, however, is not researched or explained in this text. *(Burlesque) Autobiography* hereafter cited as *BA1*.

[15]"Jack" was a shortened term for "Jackass" and Clemens in his "The Revised Catechism" would refer to "St. Ass's Colt Hall." In the winter of 1877-78 Clemens even considered writing a biography of Hall (*MTMF*, p. 219, note 1).

[16]M. R. Werner, *Tammany Hall* (Garden City, New York: Doubleday, Doran, 1931), pp. 113, 116-117.

[17]In personal correspondence, Louis J. Budd has noted that the "Harem" may also be taken at face value since Fisk was well known as a womanizer.

[18]Clemens had published the "Private Habits of Horace Greeley," in a short, humorous piece in the New York periodical *Spirit of the Times* on 7 November 1868. Source for studying Horace Greeley: Glydon G. Van Duesen, *Horace Greeley, Nineteenth-Century Crusader* (Philadelphia: University of Pennsylvania Press, 1953). Source for Charles Dana: Candace Stone, *Dana and the Sun* (New York: Dodd Mead & Company, 1938). Clemens was to have Greeley caricatured and use his *Tribune* letter as an illustration for *Roughing It* the next year.

[19]Since the Tweed ring tried to pay off the newpaper press through the official advertising of New York City, most newpapers had a tangled record of attitudes towards Tammany Hall before 1871. In "Interviewing the Interviewer," written in 1870, Clemens declared his violent dislike for Dana, accusing him of glorifying "moneyed scum" like Vanderbilt and of slandering Horace Greeley (DV 306, MTP).

[20]Judge Barnard's transactions for and against Erie are cited in detail by Charles Francis Adams, Jr., *Chapters of Erie* (Ithaca: Cornell University Press, 1956), pp. 1-100. Also in Julius Grodensky, *Jay Gould: His Business Career*, 1867-1892 (Philadelphia: University of Pennsylvania Press, 1957), pp. 40-51.

[21] Gould, Fisk, and Drew ("The Triumvirate") were inseparable in print and cartoons. However, Drew was driven from the Executive Committee early (in July of 1868) and replaced by Frederick Lane. Stephens' is accurate in his two drawings of "The Triumvirate," but less so in the rendition of Daniel Drew.

[22] *MTinEng*, p. 42.

[23] Boston *Evening Transcript*, 9 March 1871, p. 1 (*ET&S*, 1, 568).

[24] New York *Tribune*, 10 March 1871, p. 6 (*ET&S*, 1, 568).

[25] *Literary World*, I [1 April 1871]: 165. "The *Literary World's* estimate of costs was not far wrong: according to the publisher himself the paper-covered copy cost four cents to produce, the muslin-bound one only ten cents (Sheldon and Company to James R. Osgood, 19 October 1882, MTP). Sheldon had bragged in 1871 that the plates cost $400 (Orion Clemens to Clemens, 25 January 1871, MTP)" (*ET&S*, 1, 569, note 103).

[26] Sheldon to SLC, 4 April 1871, *CL* 3.

[27] "A year or two later he realized the mistake of this book, bought in the plates and destroyed them" (*MTB* I, 433). The plates of *BA*1 remained in existence, if not in use, until 1882. See *ET&S* for final disposal of the plates and remaining copies of *BA*1 (*ET&S*, 1, 570). Clemens made no arrangements for a publication of *BA*1 in London. An edition of the pamphlet was, however, pirated *without the cartoons* (*ET&S*, 1, 571-572).

List of Illustrations: *(Burlesque) Autobiography*

Fig. 1. The House that Twain built, Courtesy MTP.
Fig. 2. JACK.
Fig. 3. A. Oakey Hall, 21 October 1865, *Harper's Weekly*, Courtesy UofM.
Fig. 4. Thomas Nast, The last of the Mare Disease with which this City has been so much afflicted, Courtesy UofM.
Fig. 5. This is that House that Jack built.
Fig. 6. Whitehead, This is the Malt that Lay in the House that Jack Built, Courtesy Sinclair Hamilton Collection, Department of Rare Books and Special Collections, Princeton University Library.
Fig. 7. *(Burlesque) Autobiography*, This is the Malt that lay in the House that Jack built.
Fig. 8. This is the Rat that ate the Malt that lay in the House that Jack built.
Fig. 9. JAMES FISK, JUN., 16 October 1869, *Harper's Weekly*, Courtesy UofM.
Fig. 10. Thomas Nast, WHAT I KNOW ABOUT HORACE GREELEY, 10 November 1866, *Harper's Weekly.* Courtesy UofM.
Fig. 11. This is the Cat that caught the rat that ate the malt that lay in the House that Jack built.
Fig. 12. CHARLES DANA, Courtesy MTP.
Fig. 13. This is the Dog that "worried" the cat that caught the rat that ate the malt that lay in the House that Jack built.
Fig. 14. This is the Cow with the crumpled horn that tossed the dog that worried the cat that caught the rat that ate the malt that lay in the House that Jack built.
Fig. 15. MESSRS. FISK AND GOULD ESCAPING TO NEW JERSEY. 11 April 1868, *Harper's Weekly*, Courtesy MTP.
Fig. 16. THE ERIE RAILROAD DIRECTORS' ROOM AT THE TAYLOR HOTEL. JERSEY CITY. 11 April

1868, *Harper's Weekly*, Courtesy MTP.

Fig. 17.   This is the Maiden all forlorn that milked the cow with the crumpled horn that tossed the dog that worried the cat that caught the rat that ate the malt that lay in the House that Jack built.

Fig. 18.   JUDGE GEORGE BARNARD. Courtesy Berg Collection, New York Public Library.

Fig. 19.   This is the Man all "tattered and torn" that loved the maiden all forlorn that milked the cow with the crumpled horn that tossed the dog that worried the cat that caught the rat that ate the malt that lay in the House that Jack built.

Fig. 20.   DANIEL DREW, 11 April 1868, *Harper's Weekly*, Courtesy MTP.

Fig. 21.   PETER "BRAINS" SWEENEY, 4 December 1869, *Harper's Weekly*, Courtesy MTP.

Fig. 22.   CORNELIUS VANDERBILT, 11 April 1868, *Harper's Weekly*, Courtesy MTP.

Fig. 23.   This is the Priest (not) shaven and shorn, that married the man all tattered and torn unto the maiden all forlorn that milked the cow with the crumpled horn that tossed the dog that worried the cat that caught the rat that ate the malt that lay in the House that Jack built.

Fig. 24.   HON. WILLIAM M. TWEED, 21 January 1871, *Harper's Weekly*, Courtesy MTP.

Fig. 25.   Thomas Nast, THE POWER BEHIND THE THRONE, 29 October 1870, *Harper's Weekly*, Courtesy UofM.

Fig. 26.   JAY GOULD, Courtesy Brown Brothers.

Fig. 27.   This is the Cock that crowed in the morn to wake (into existence) the man all tattered and torn that married the maiden all forlorn that milked the cow with the crumpled horn that tossed the dog that worried the cat that caught the rat that ate the malt that lay in the House that Jack built.

Fig. 28.   HON. JOHN T. HOFFMAN, MAYOR-ELECT OF NEW YORK CITY, 23 December 1865, *Harper's Weekly*, Courtesy UofM.

Chapter III

Roughing It

"The fault is mainly in the engravings."

Though *(Burlesque) Autobiography* had a lasting effect on Mark Twain's conception of design, the pamphlet was a mere interlude in the author's publishing career. His principal desire was to repeat the success of *The Innocents Abroad.* Toward this end he and Bliss signed a formal contract for another subscription book. Illustration was an integral part of the agreement: "The American Publishing Company agree to publish the said book in their best style. . ., being well done in text and illustrations."[1] Since the travel book *The Innocents Abroad* had been a best seller, Twain doubted whether he "could do better than rub up old Pacific memories & put them between covers along with some eloquent pictures."[2] Gone were all his questions on whether or not to include engravings; Twain now regarded them as vital to any book he would publish. He wrote to his brother Orion, who was now both a Bliss editor for *The American Publisher* and a handy man around the office, "I am to the 570th page and booming along." In the previous paragraph he had urged Orion to "tell Bliss to hatch up lots of pictures for the book—it is going to sell bully."[3] A month later he wrote, "I have enough manuscript on hand now to make (allowing for engravings) about four hundred pages of the book."[4]

In almost every letter during the hectic months of writing *Roughing It,* Mark Twain expressed his need for illustration: "If I get only half a chance I will write a book that will sell like fury provided you [Bliss] put pictures enough in it."[5] "This book will be pretty readable, after all; and if it is well and profusely illustrated it will crowd the 'Innocents.' "[6] "It will be a starchy book, and should be full of snappy pictures—especially pictures worked in with the letterpress."[7] Pictures, pages, and profits now had a direct correlation for him.

Since the format for *The Innocents Abroad* had drawn such favorable reviews, Mark Twain and his editor saw no reason to disturb the pattern. The types of illustration in the first book were worked into the pages of the second, this being standard subscription practice: original photographs of famous people were used as portraits; caricatures of Twain and others in the story were distributed here and there in the letter press; and framable engravings of frontier locations were sprinkled liberally through the signatures.

Bliss perceived one necessary change for the book; he immediately began a search for a new illustrator. He was less concerned about the quality of True Williams' work than about his sobriety, which was constantly in question. Hiring a more temperate artist would alleviate this worry. Bliss, after careful consultation, decided to contact Edward F. Mullen.

As stated in the previous chapter, Mullen's name had come up when Clemens was negotiating with Bliss for the publication of his sketches and for work on *(Burlesque) Autobiography*. He had written to Bliss, "You must illustrate it *[Sketchbook]* —& mind you, the man to do the choicest of the pictures is Mullin [sic] —the Sisters are reforming him & he is sadly in need of work & money."[8]

The semi-reformed inebriate was hardly the ideal substitute for a tippling Williams. But since he had previously worked for Bliss, creating at least two cuts for Richardson's *Beyond the Mississippi,* and since the publisher had Clemens' word that the Sisters were in control, Bliss endeavored to make contact. The comic details of his attempts were related to Clemens by his brother, Orion, who was fast becoming a conduit of gossipy information between the author and his editor. Orion wrote Clemens this disconnected note:

> He [Bliss] hunted for Mullin [sic] and Lant Thompson, or whatever his name is, two days. He found the . . . office in the hands of plasterers. He is going back to-morrow and will find Mullin . . . . A New York engraver had just come in. He says he has a judgment against Mullin . . . Bliss charges him [the engraver] with pawning blocks for whiskey and charging fancy prices without doing them better. . . . Still, he [Bliss] says he is going to get him [Mullen] to do some work.[9]

Mullen was found and hired but not as the principal illustrator. He worked at least four cuts for the book, each signed E F M. It is probable, too, that some of the pictures in

AN ENEMY'S PRAYER.

Fig. 1. AN ENEMY'S PRAYER.

the Sandwich Islands chapters are his since they match his style (Fig. 1).[10]

At about the same time Bliss decided to return to True Williams as the major artist: he was available, had behaved fairly responsibly on the first book, and was probably not too expensive.

With two of the illustrators agreed upon, Bliss encouraged Mark Twain to press on with the manuscript. He desperately needed copy to get up the *Roughing It* prospectus. The subscription sales market depended almost entirely on an army of canvassing agents going door-to-door displaying the prospectus: a bound copy of excerpted text with hundreds of illustrations from the still unprinted book. The prospectus included an ornate title page, a fairly complete table of contents, pages of text, and a major share of the pictures, along with various choices in bindings. Bliss wanted his agents to start their rounds immediately to exploit the success of *The Innocents Abroad*. He was, however, stymied. Twain was not producing manuscript. The author had found that without the handy backlog of already written material—like the *Alta* letters for *The Innocents Abroad*—writing a massive travel yarn about vaguely remembered incidents was a formidable task. Furthermore, he had also contracted to write for *Galaxy* and *The American Publisher*. His stock of creative ideas was running dry. Nevertheless, Bliss continued to plead for more copy.

In mid-May 1871 Bliss wrote to Clemens:

> We intend to do *our part* towards making your book what
> it should be in illustrations. We shall try to have just the
> kind in that will suit, and think we shall succeed. I
> think it would be well to have Prospectus out *soon as
> practicable* as agents are anxious for it.[11]

By July Bliss was writing again about illustration and
frantically asking his author at least to give the book a title.

> Would like all the Mss. you have to be able to select
> subjects for *full page engravings*—want all I can of these
> to go in the Prospectus. . . . What is to be the title—
> this is a matter of some importance you know, and
> necessary for the Prospectus, unless we say we don't
> know it yet and call it the *"Unnamed"* and wait for
> developments to christen it.[12]

When there was no answer from Clemens, Bliss took matters
into his own hands and titled the book *Roughing It.*[13] He continued having the illustrators work on subjects from the manuscript on hand.

A drawing of Mark Twain on stage, SEVERE CASE OF
STAGE-FRIGHT, was possibly one of the first completed
sketches for the book. It was drawn for the San Francisco
lecture anecdote, Chapter LXXVIII, which had been included in
early material. This engraving was placed in the Prospectus and
Bliss also used it on circulars and advertisements. Whereas in
The Innocents Abroad Twain had been touted as the foolish
traveler-tourist (see Chapter 1), now, to promote *Roughing It,*
he was being depicted as the bumbling lecturer (Fig. 2).

Receiving a copy of the first prospectus, Clemens expressed
his pleasure to Olivia (now his wife): "I think Bliss has gotten
up the prospectus book with taste & skill."[14] Unfortunately,
with the completion of the sample copy Bliss's problems were
not ended. Though the prospectus was in the agents' hands and
orders for the book were coming in, the book itself was far from
complete and a major share of the drawings were unfinished.

To complicate matters, in the fall of 1871 Clemens' new
life style forced him into an extended lecture tour—his expenses
had risen appreciably since his marriage. He had by no means
put the book out of his mind, for his speeches contained seg-
ments from his forthcoming work (Figs. 3 & 4).[15] However, his

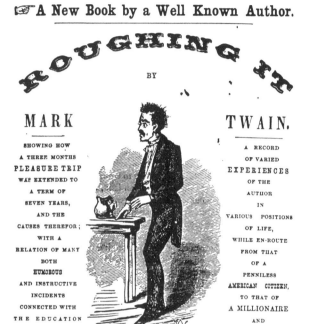

☞ **A New Book by a Well Known Author.**

ROUGHING IT

BY

MARK TWAIN.

SHOWING HOW
A THREE MONTHS
PLEASURE TRIP
WAS EXTENDED TO
A TERM OF
SEVEN YEARS,
AND THE
CAUSES THEREFOR;
WITH A
RELATION OF MANY
BOTH
HUMOROUS
AND INSTRUCTIVE
INCIDENTS
CONNECTED WITH
THE EDUCATION
OF AN
INNOCENT

A RECORD
OF VARIED
EXPERIENCES
OF THE
AUTHOR
IN
VARIOUS POSITIONS
OF LIFE,
WHILE EN-ROUTE
FROM THAT
OF A
PENNILESS
AMERICAN CITIZEN,
TO THAT OF
A MILLIONAIRE
AND
BACK TO HIS
ORIGINAL CONDITION

Hundreds of Characteristic Engravings

EXECUTED BY SOME OF THE

BEST ARTISTS IN THE LAND

ADD INTEREST TO THE TEXT.

THE VOLUME WILL CONSIST OF

Nearly 600 Octavo Pages,

AND WILL BE FOUND TO CONTAIN NOT ONLY MATTER OF AN AMUSING CHARACTER, BUT
TO BE A VALUABLE AND CORRECT HISTORY OF AN INTENSELY INTERESTING PERIOD,
WITH LUDICROUS DESCRIPTIONS OF SCENES NEVER BEFORE WRITTEN UP.

Fig. 2. Prospectus, *Roughing It.*

lecturing, though it brought in some much-needed money, contributed to the delay in the publication of *Roughing It.* Bliss
and his subordinates in the office were left to make all the remaining decisions for the book: correcting text, choosing
drawings for insertion, proofreading the galleys and print pages,
etc. Naively, Clemens believed that Bliss would handle all the
monotonous details of production, keeping the financial interests
of the author, rather than the company, as first priority.
Clemens would soon learn that Bliss was a salesman, not a saint.

When the first batch of drawings arrived at the publishing
office, Bliss recruited Orion Clemens to ferret out inconsistencies
in story and illustration and to proofread text. He was the
perfect choice since he had been to Nevada with his brother, and

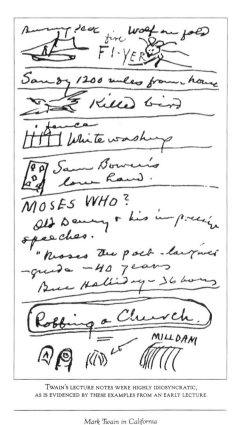

TWAIN'S LECTURE NOTES WERE HIGHLY IDIOSYNCRATIC,
AS IS EVIDENCED BY THESE EXAMPLES FROM AN EARLY LECTURE.

Mark Twain in California

Fig. 3. Mark Twain's Lecture Notes.

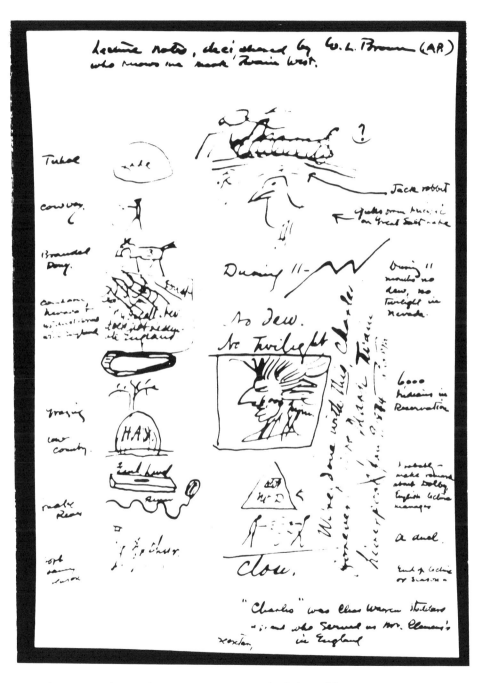

Fig. 4. Mark Twain's Lecture Notes, deciphered by W. L. Brown.

much of the material in the book had been borrowed from Orion's journals. Orion performed his job judiciously, often reporting by letter to Clemens on the book's progress.

> Some of the artists' drafts for the pictures have come. I told Frank [Elisha Bliss's son] to take the tree out of Carson and put the auctioneer on the horse. He said he would take the tree out, but people here wouldn't understand the idea of an auctioneer on a horse. Another [print] has him taking his rider over a pile of telegraph poles—another bucking—and another going through a gate, raking his rider off the top beam. He is a ragged looking horse.[16]

Orion's note to Clemens provides several clues to an illustrator's working habits and the ensuing problems. Illustrators of the time were, as Clemens would find out, notoriously poor manuscript readers. If they had carefully read the Carson section they would have understood that there was "not a tree in sight" and that Nevada had "no vegetation but the endless sage-brush and greasewood."[17] When Orion pointed out the facts, Frank ordered the artists to cut all trees in the Nevada chapters.

The series of drawings under discussion must have been part of the Mexican Plug chapter. The original sketches of which Orion writes were undoubtedly redrawn since, like the Carson City trees, the telegraph poles and gates were dropped. The sequence, revised and finally printed in the first edition, serves as an example of the inferior quality of illustration throughout *Roughing It*. Mark Twain's idea for the book had been to extend the western "tall-tale": taking a simple story, or series of stories, and piling exaggeration upon exaggeration to the point of absurdity. The buying of the Plug was just such an exaggerated story.

When first introducing the reader to the odd-looking animal, Twain had written: "The auctioneer came skurrying through the plaza on a black beast that had as many humps and corners on him as a dromedary, and was necessarily uncomely."[18] Twain's buying the angular creature was, after this description, sheer comedy. Frank Bliss's comment from the letter was logical: an eastern audience might not comprehend a mounted auctioneer. But the younger Bliss had missed the point. The horse, not the auctioneer, was the important element in the anecdote. Lack of

"YOU MIGHT THINK HIM AN AMERICAN HORSE."

"YOU MIGHT THINK HIM AN AMERICAN HORSE."
Fig. 5.

UNEXPECTED ELEVATION.

Fig. 6. UNEXPECTED ELEVATION.

UNIVERSALLY UNSETTLED.

Fig. 7. UNIVERSALLY UNSETTLED.

RIDING THE PLUG.

Fig. 8. RIDING THE PLUG.

WANTED EXERCISE.

Fig. 9. WANTED EXERCISE.

logic, irrationality, is what makes a tall-tale work. Eventually the illustrator redrew the auctioneer appropriately seated, but the horse remained merely "ragged looking," not ridiculous (Fig. 5).

Taking the cuts in the order of final printing, we infer that Orion's reference to "another bucking" was undoubtedly the next print where Mark Twain takes his first ride on his newly purchased Mexican Plug. The print shows a surprised fellow (a caricature of Twain) a foot in the air off the saddle. It is the best illustration in the sequence (Fig. 6). To jibe with Twain's text the next cut should have the unhorsed rider sitting down on a stone.[19] The reader, however, sees not a seat of stone but a log (Fig. 7). And when the Plug finally rushes off with the Speaker of the House, Twain writes, "the first dash the creature made was over a pile of telegraph poles half as high as a church."[20] Obviously the original sketch Orion saw with telegraph poles was accurate. But the reworked and finally printed cut has the horse easily leaping over a "split-rail" fence, the Speaker losing his hat but remaining in the saddle (Fig. 8).

Each individual factual flaw is irrelevant. However, the building and connecting of each separate, absurd detail is the very essence of Mark Twain's tall-tale. The picture sequence does not build. The drawings are ordinary, not foolish; dull, not comical. They needed the punch of, say, the outrageous "Old Masters" in *The Innocents Abroad.* Here the same illustrator (Williams) is not only inaccurate but, more important, unsympathetic to Twain's narrative style.

The last drawing for this Plug series, WANTED EXERCISE, fits perfectly into the sequence. Mark Twain's text speaks of an unhorsed rider dejectedly walking home from the wild ride. What is puzzling about the picture is the signature, "Richardson," clearly visible in the left-hand corner of the print. Richardson had been one of the engravers for Albert Richardson's *Beyond the Mississippi.* And, interestingly, this particular print originally had been drawn for the Mississippi book by Henry Stephens, Twain's illustrator for *(Burlesque) Autobiography.* Another Stephens-drawn, Richardson-engraved cut from *Beyond the Mississippi* appears as A HIGH PRIVATE—TAIL-PIECE, in *Roughing It.* In a manner of speaking, therefore, Stephens did some illustrating for *Roughing It.*[21] The tangled mysteries of Bliss's acquisition of these and other prints for the book unfold as more of the drawings are examined (Figs. 9 & 10).

Fig. 10. A HIGH PRIVATE—TAIL-PIECE.

Meanwhile, Bliss and his assistants were working with *The Innocents Abroad* as their model and trying to adhere to their highest subscription standards. Both portraits and caricatures were appropriately inserted into the letterpress, though much less effectively than in Mark Twain's earlier book. Only two people were depicted in portraiture, Heber C. Kimball and Brigham Young. Neither actually warranted a portrait. Each man is referred to in only one line in this chapter—though Young is frequently satirized in the next section. Pictures of the two men appear facing each other on pages 112 and 113, with Young's portrait the larger of the two (Figs. 11 & 12). It may be that the chief reason for the inclusion of these two prints was that Bliss had them handy in his files.

PORTRAIT OF
HEBER KIMBALL.
Fig. 11

PORTRAIT OF
BRIGHAM YOUNG.
Fig. 12

Using fewer portraits than in *The Innocents Abroad* may have been dictated by the different nature of the narrative. Kings, queens, and emperors bulk fairly large in *The Innocents Abroad*, and their portraits are not out of place there. Not so in *Roughing It*. Yet Bliss must have had plates of a number of the mentioned notables: Governor Nye of Nevada, Reuel Gridley of the "Sanitary Flour Sack" episode, or Horace Greeley, whose undecipherable letter and "bald-headed" ride form two of the most amusing chapters in *Roughing It*. Just why the book has so few cuts featuring real people in portraiture remains a mystery.

A caricature of Horace Greeley and his *Tribune* letter were both featured illustrations in the book. Though the original Greeley letter had spoken practically about potatoes and cabbages, Mark Twain's version produced a comical translation about turnips and polygamy. The 1871 letter offering advice about potato planting probably served as model for the full-page print, making it easy for the artists to replicate the *Tribune* letterhead, the closing, and Greeley's signature. There is evidence that the illegible imitation of Greeley's letter may have been supplied by Twain when he mailed the manuscript to Hartford.[22] Obviously, Greeley's scrawl needed little alteration to achieve to the illegibility Mark Twain described in his anecdote (Figs. 13 & 14).

Horace Greeley's features again were caricatured as they had been in *(Burlesque) Autobiography* and, interestingly, the artists also made an effort to capture the facial features of the legendary stage coach driver, Hank Monk (Figs. 15 & 16).

A number of other recognizable characters were also caricatured: Calvin Higbie, the short-term millionaire to whom Mark Twain dedicated the book (Figs. 17 & 18); Jim Gillis, the pocket-miner and superb story-teller who had handed on to Twain some of the delightful tales used in *Roughing It* (Figs. 19 & 20); and Dan De Quille, Clemens' clever, hard-drinking friend and fellow reporter on the *Territorial Enterprise* (Figs. 21 & 22).[23]

Mark Twain's features, of course, appear most often in the drawings—forty-four times, give or take a few unrecognizable cuts. By this time the author was certainly no stranger to his readers and therefore the artists had real reason to use his image liberally. Twain, on the other hand, seemed to crave more and better exposure. In early correspondence with Orion he had boasted: "As I am now unquestionably notorious, it will be

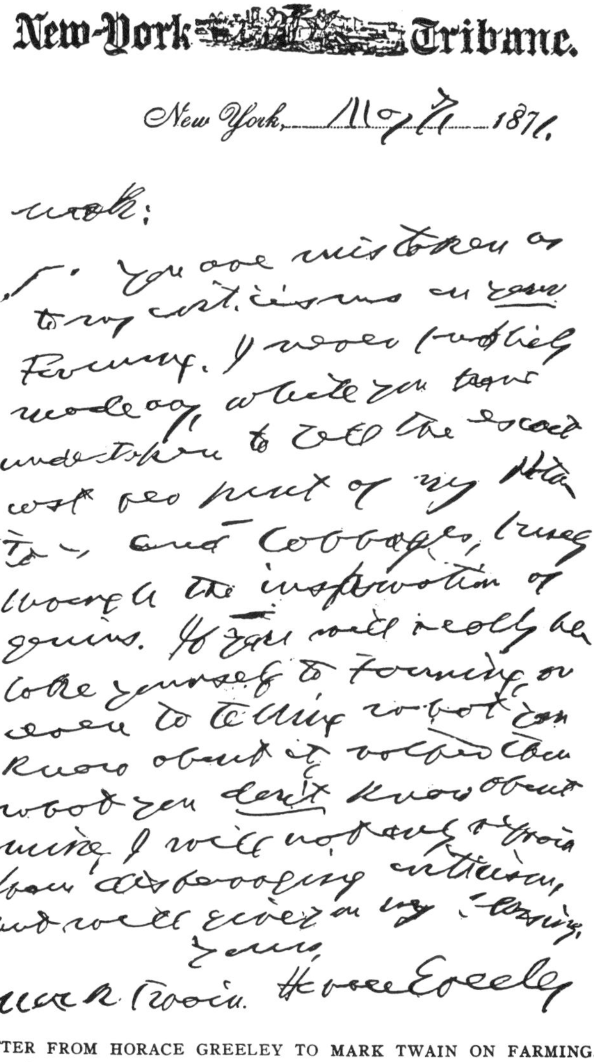

LETTER FROM HORACE GREELEY TO MARK TWAIN ON FARMING.
PROBABLY USED AS THE MODEL FOR THE GREELEY
FACSIMILE IN "ROUGHING IT"

LETTER FROM HORACE GREELEY TO MARK TWAIN ON
FARMING.
Fig. 13.

HORACE GREELEY—HIS MARK. 509

New-York Tribune.

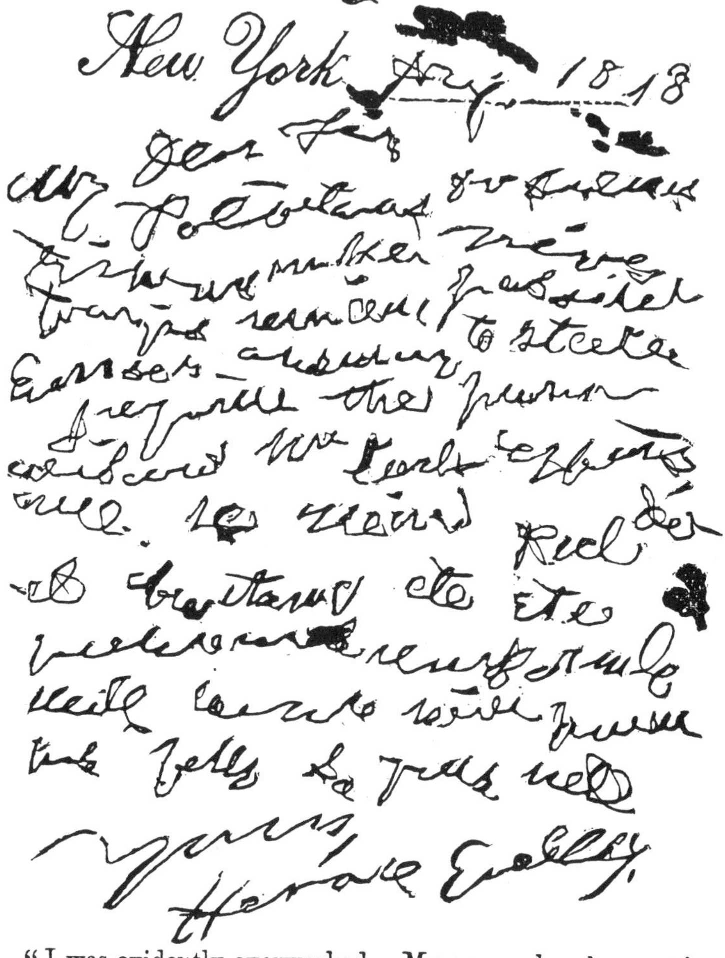

"I was evidently overworked. My comprehension was impaired. Therefore I gave two days to recreation, and then returned to my task greatly refreshed. The letter now took this form:

'Poultices do sometimes choke swine; tulips reduce posterity; causes leather to resist. Our notions empower wisdom, her let's afford while we can. Butter but any cakes, fill any undertaker, we'll wean him from his filly. We feel hot.

Yrxwly, HEVACE EVEELOJ.'

Fig. 14. HORACE GREELEY LETTER, *Roughing It.*

GREELEY'S RIDE.

Fig. 15. GREELEY'S RIDE.

"My delight, the driver." This is Hank Monk, known as the prince of stage drivers. He worked for Wells Fargo. Drivers drew salaries as high as $250 a month —the salary Mark Twain got as river pilot.

Fig. 16. Hank Monk, Wells Fargo Stage Driver.

MILLIONAIRES LAYING PLANS.

Fig. 17. MILLIONAIRES LAYING PLANS.

Fig. 18. Calvin Higbie.

INCIPIENT MILLIONAIRES.

Fig. 19. INCIPIENT MILLIONAIRES.

Fig. 20. Jim Gillis.

DISSOLUTE AUTHOR.

Fig. 21. DISSOLUTE AUTHOR.

Fig. 22. Dan De Quille.

justifiable to have a steel portrait of the author in the new book—
if not in late editions of the Innocents."[24]

Bliss, already spending a good deal of time and money on
illustration, didn't want or need the complication of producing a
steel engraving of Mark Twain for a frontispiece. The portrait,
for whatever reason, did not appear in *Roughing It* nor in the
later editions of *The Innocents Abroad.* Twain's subsequent
books, however, did include full-page engraved portraits of the
author, usually placed opposite the frontispiece, and usually
insisted upon by Twain.

With Bliss and the artists so dedicated to caricature as the
principal style of illustration for *Roughing It*, it seems strange
that a most important picture, that of Senator Stewart, was
inserted as an undistinguished and even inaccurate cut. There
was no doubt concerning Clemens' attitude toward the man or
the need for a likeness of him in the book. Stewart and Clemens
had met in Washington in 1867 and 1869 when the Senator represented Nevada in the Capitol. They had roomed in the same
house and Clemens had even, for a very short time, served as the
Senator's secretary.[25]

The Stewart episode in *Roughing It* featured a fictional and
irrational stock swindle. According to Mark Twain's story, he
had refused an offered gift of stock certificates from a "Mr.
Stewart (Senator, now, from Nevada)."[26] In the next paragraph, Twain told how he later found that these same certificates
had increased in value, and how he had—quite logically, he
thought—decided now to accept the stocks and the dividends
from the Senator. When Stewart refused (unreasonably
according to the author!) an injured Twain pouts self-righteous-
ly: "I suppose he sold that stock of mine and placed the guilty
proceeds in his own pocket. [My revenge will be found in the
accompanying portrait.]"[27] Apparently Mark Twain had
wanted a portrait—or at least a good likeness—of Stewart inserted just here since he had so pointedly directed his reader's
attention to a picture. However, a ridiculous caricature which
bore little or no resemblance to Stewart was placed on the same
page as the anecdote about the casually refused stock, and on the
following page was depicted a top-hatted, clean-shaven, middle-
aged male with an eye-patch.[28] The portrait is captioned POR-
TRAIT OF MR. STEWART, but the face has none of the
features of the famous Senator (Figs. 23, 24, & 25).

The "List of Illustrations" cites a PORTRAIT OF SEN-

ATOR STEWART, a label similar to those used for the portraits of Kimball and Young. It seems a reasonable conjecture that an actual portrait, like those of Kimball and Young, was originally planned. The "List" was apparently completed before all the cuts were finished, and through some oversight the intended portrait was omitted.

"TRY A FEW?"

Fig. 23. "TRY A FEW?"

PORTRAIT OF MR. STEWART.

Fig. 24. PORTRAIT OF MR. STEWART.

Senator William M. Stewart of Nevada. Mark Twain
was his private secretary briefly in 1867. When Stewart wrote his memoirs, he did not remember Mark
fondly.

Fig. 25. Senator William M. Stewart.

The failure of the caricature was either another instance of inattentiveness on the part of the illustrator or a communication gap between the author, editor, and the artist. Whatever the explanation, the Stewart illustrations were badly off target and gave Clemens only a modicum of his desired revenge.

As it turned out, Senator Stewart did feel insulted. In his memoirs he charged that "In *Roughing It* Mark Twain had accused him of cheating, had printed a scurrilous 'portrait' and had claimed to have given him a thrashing."[29] Evidently a few of Twain's barbs had struck home, however badly aimed.

With a good many of the drawings still incomplete, Williams, unfortunately, fell back into his old habits. Reports drifted in to Bliss that Williams was on a spree. He had been seen climbing a lamppost outside Dooley's saloon, offering to go to the top to amuse the spectators if they would buy him a drink.

Bliss began to panic. The longer the publication date was delayed the more Twain's readers would forget their pleasure from *The Innocents Abroad*; the market for a new book would dwindle away. With Williams on a binge, Bliss turned to Roswell Morse Shurtleff, who had done a few scenes for *The Innocents*

THE MINER'. DREAM.

Fig. 26. THE MINER'S DREAM.

Fig. 27. THE SOUTH PASS.

Abroad, to do some of the remaining drawings. At the time Shurtleff was entering a new phase of his career, oil painting, and was furiously completing canvases for a first exhibition at the National Academy. However, he accepted Bliss's offer and did fill-in work on *Roughing It*, creating two important full-page prints: THE MINER'S DREAM (which Bliss used as a frontispiece) and THE SOUTH PASS. In addition to these he sketched and signed seventeen other cuts; there are also many unsigned prints in the first edition which suggest Shurtleff's style (Figs. 26 & 27).[30]

It was now winter. Bliss realized that if he waited much longer to issue the book, agents' orders would never reach their customers by Christmas. Bliss, therefore, took the first pre-publication step and deposited the title page with the Library of Congress on 6 December 1871—a somewhat chancey step, since at that late date many illustrations were not finished. Bliss complained that he had "set up to page 300 but plates not finished of yet. They [the engravers] are finishing as we have begun to print. We are kept back by here and there a cut not yet done."[31]

Examination of the design in the first American edition of *Roughing It* reveals not only inaccurate and unsympathetic art work but also the usual inconsistency of style; a clear result of Bliss's commissioning a semi-reformed Mullen, a recidivous Williams, and a preoccupied Shurtleff. But some of the shadier aspects of Bliss's *modus operandi* also contributed to this inconsistency.

Bliss, under time pressures, had resorted to rather drastic measures not unusual in the subscription business, to speed up the illustrating delay. He worried little about the ethics of his decision. Clemens was away on his lecture tour and Bliss's son, Frank, was supervising the proofreading in the company office. Bliss overlooked Orion Clemens, who was also doing some proofreading. Orion proved to be both curious about the book's design and loyal to his brother's interests.

The engraving company for *Roughing It*, noted on the "List of Illustrations," was again Fay and Cox. Specific engravers' names were not noted—although engravers were often credited in American Publishing Company's books. Examination of the cuts and their signatures reveals a number of suspicious markings: Roberts, Lauderback, Langridge, Richardson, P, and T. M. Each of these signatures, excluding the initials, were the markings of well-known engravers or engraving firms in the publishing busi-ess of the time.[32]   Coincidentally, both Richardson and Lan-gridge had engraved plates for *Beyond the Mississippi*. Since Bliss had borrowed the Stephens plate WANTED EXERCISE from this book, it seems logical to suspect that he might have borrowed others. A comparison of the prints from both books confirms this suspicion: the Langridge cut (originally drawn by J. C. Beard) is found on page 147 of *Roughing It* and page 495 of *Beyond the Mississippi* (Fig. 28).

GOSHOOT INDIANS HANGING AROUND STATIONS.
GOSHOOT INDIANS HANGING AROUND STATIONS.
Fig. 28

Continuing the search, one discovers that the illustrators' work was as freely and casually exchanged as was that of en-gravers. Though a vast number of the cuts in *Roughing It* have the familiar Williams logo—T over W placed in the right-hand corner—Shurtleff's S or Rs and Mullen's E F M command their share as well. But there are still other artists' signatures—Warren, for instance. Warren must indicate A. Coolidge Warren, a Boston illustrator who had sketched twenty-three cuts for *Beyond the Mississippi*. The capital P and T. M. markings are at this time unidentifiable.[33]

Obviously, with time an imperative, Bliss had reached for the most convenient, already engraved plates he could find from his stock of previously printed material. Plates most frequently borrowed for use in *Roughing It* were taken from Albert Richardson's *Beyond the Mississippi*, Thomas Knox's *Overland Through Asia*, and John Ross Browne's *Adventures in the Apache Country: A Tour Through Arizona and Sonora.*[34]

Bliss had only to leaf through Knox, Richardson, and Browne to find enough appropriate or sufficiently ambiguous prints to fill his *Roughing It* needs. Three prints from Knox and fourteen from Richardson were hustled into the type-high plates and printed. It was certainly a practical solution, since Bliss had published Knox in 1870 and brought out a second printing of Richardson in 1869, almost the same years he was supervising the *Roughing It* manuscript. Fortunately for Bliss, the subject matter was also often identical: Nevada locations, quartz mining, Mormon customs, and the problems with the Chinese. In fact, Clemens himself had commented in a letter to Orion on the parallels: "Knox had printed a similar story (the same 'situation' has been in print often—men have written it before Knox and I were born)."[35]

Clemens was also aware and most appreciative of the work of J. Ross Browne. As early as 1862 he had suggested to his mother that if she was curious about the Nevada territory she should look at Browne's pictures in the *Harper's Monthly* of the period. Clemens was even personally acquainted with the author-artist: in 1866 he had stayed with the Browne family during his California lecture tour.[36] Many scholars have since observed that Mark Twain's writing style was reminiscent of, or had been influenced by, Browne's travel narratives.[37]

In Bliss's borrowing of illustrations from J. Ross Browne's *Adventures in the Apache Country* the method of transfer from book to book shifts. The publishing dates are close together (1869 for *Adventures* and 1872 for *Roughing It*), but the publisher of the Browne book was Harper and Brothers. Thus Bliss would not have had ready access to the plates. How or why Bliss came to use the Browne prints—they were all drawn by the author—may never be known.

It is a fact, however, that though Bliss usually removed neither the engraver's nor the illustrator's name, in many instances he did have his engravers alter the plates. Of the five prints used from Browne, only one was an exact duplicate: BATTERY AND AMALGAMATION ROOM (recaptioned ANOTHER PROCESS OF AMALGAMATION, Fig. 29). Four others were altered: MONO LAKE (recaptioned LAKE MONO with

human figures added to the Twain print, Figs. 30 & 31);
ARIZONIAN IN SIGHT OF HOME (recaptioned THE SAVED
BROTHER, with a staff replacing the arrow, Figs. 32 & 33);
STAND FROM UNDER (recaptioned NO PARTICULAR
HURRY, Figs. 34 & 35); and ONE OF THE CANDIDATES FOR
MAYOR (recaptioned THE MAN WHO HAD KILLED A
DOZEN, Figs. 36 & 37), the latter two greatly changed.[38]

ANOTHER PROCESS OF AMALGAMATION.

Fig. 29. ANOTHER PROCESS OF AMALGAMATION.

MONO LAKE.

Fig. 30. MONO LAKE.

Fig. 31. LAKE MONO.

ARIZONIAN IN SIGHT OF HOME.

THE SAVED BROTHER.

ARIZONIAN IN SIGHT OF HOME.   THE SAVED BROTHER.
Fig. 32.   Fig. 33.

STAND FROM UNDER!
Fig. 34.

NO PARTICULAR HURRY.
Fig. 35.

ONE OF THE CANDIDATES FOR MAYOR.

Fig. 36. ONE OF THE CANDIDATES FOR MAYOR.

THE MAN WHO HAD KILLED A DOZEN.

Fig. 37. THE MAN WHO HAD KILLED A DOZEN.

Modifications were also performed on three plates originally drawn by A. W. Waud for *Beyond the Mississippi*, each change made to better fit the content of Mark Twain's story.[39] Waud's OUR HOUSE IN DENVER was cut in half (eliminating the house and leaving only the animals) and recaptioned PRAIRIE DOGS (Figs. 38 & 39). A cut captioned THE AUTHOR ARRIVES IN DENVER had, appropriately, the face of Richardson as the horseback rider in his book. Engravers removed the head and replaced it with the face of a soulfully scowling drifter and, recaptioned MAGNIFICENCE AND MISERY, it was printed in *Roughing It* (Figs. 40 & 41). One other print, A STATE OF SUSPENSE, served as a tail piece for Twain's chapter—no need for a caption—but had a changed banner on the corpse. Richardson's victim had been hanged by vigilantes and wore a sign MURDERER; Twain's character was a mere prevaricator who, having hanged himself, wore the sign LIAR (Figs. 42 & 43).

OUR HOUSE IN DENVER.

Fig. 38. OUR HOUSE IN DENVER.

PRAIRIE DOGS.

Fig. 39. PRAIRIE DOGS.

THE AUTHOR ARRIVES IN DENVER.

MAGNIFICENCE AND MISERY.

THE AUTHOR ARRIVES
IN DENVER.
Fig. 40.

MAGNIFICENCE AND
MISERY.
Fig. 41.

A STATE OF SUSPENSE.

Fig. 42. A STATE OF SUSPENSE.   Fig. 43. TAIL-PIECE.

One cut, Chinese lettering rather than a real picture, showed Bliss's ingenuity in using existing plates. In the chapter on the industrious Chinese of San Francisco, Mark Twain again had directed his reader's attention to a specific drawing that was this time inserted below his text:

> The chief employment of Chinamen in towns is to wash clothing. They always send a bill, *like this below,* pinned to the clothes. It is mere ceremony, for it does not enlighten the customer much. [Italics mine][40]

Both customer and reader needed enlightening. The "bill," cited in the "List of Illustrations" as a CHINESE WASH BILL, was actually not a bill at all, but rather, according to Richardson's book where it was first printed, an INVITATION TO CHINESE DINNER.

Bliss changed Richardson's invitation by having the engraver use the last section (row 1, the salutation in Chinese), which means "May Mr. Lieh prosper," adding a character from the first line (row 4), which means in Chinese "light," a term of respect much like our "Honorable"—then simply discarded the rest of the lettering.   In the transposition, the printer unknowingly turned the character for "light" sideways.   The fact that the design was a courteous, though inaccurate, greeting rather than a laundry bill was presumably immaterial to most of Mark Twain's readers (Figs. 44 & 45).

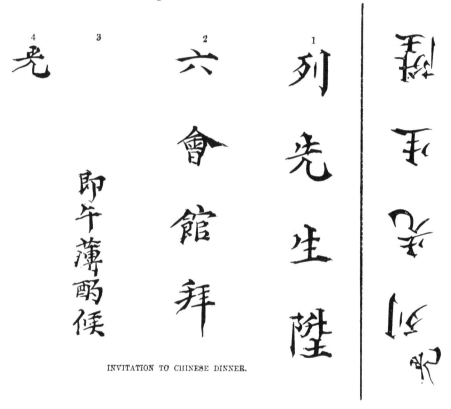

INVITATION TO CHINESE DINNER.

INVITATION TO CHINESE DINNER.   CHINESE WASH BILL.
Fig. 44.   Fig. 45.

Another cut concerning the Chinese, this time a picture taken unchanged from Thomas Knox's book, was used as a tail piece for this same chapter. The drawing shows a rather startling scene which is described only in Knox:

> The peddlers have fruit and other edibles, not omitting
> an occasional string of rats suspended from bamboo
> poles, and attached to cards on which the prices, and

sometimes the excellent qualities of the rodents, are set forth. . . . The Chinese are greatly slandered on the rat question. As a people they are not given to eating these little animals; it is only among the poorer classes that they are tolerated. . . . I was always suspicious when the Chinese urged me to partake of little meat pies.[41]

Captioned in Knox PROVISION DEALER, the drawing was cited in Mark Twain's book in the "List of Illustrations" as CHINESE MERCHANT AT HOME—TAIL PIECE. How the cut found its way into *Roughing It* proves as interesting a story as the one about the Chinese Wash Bill (Fig. 46).

CHINESE MERCHANT AT HOME—TAIL PIECE.
Fig. 46.

Years before, Mark Twain had written a column for the *Virginia City Enterprise* in which he had included clichés about the Chinese and their involvement in lotteries, prostitution, and rodents. In revising the *Enterprise* columns for his Eastern audience, Twain retained the section on the lottery but deleted the material on prostitution. He also included only two brief references to Chinese cuisine in *Roughing It*: "[the Chinaman] feasts on succulent rats and birds'-nests in Paradise," and, "He offered us. . .small, neat sausages. . .but we suspected that each link contained the corpse of a mouse."[42]

When the last page of the chapter was set by the compositors too much white space was left on it. A tail piece was needed. Bliss supplied Knox's Chinese merchant to save time and money. Mark Twain's reaction to this drawing is not on record, so far as we know. Whether he found this print a huge joke, or whether he saw in it a blatant racism out of all proportion to his reference to "the corpse of a mouse" is a matter for speculation.

Two additional cuts from the Knox book were also used in *Roughing It* as tail pieces though they were not as neatly relevant to the story as the oriental rat seller. These prints, and a number of similarly styled drawings found in most subscription books, were called "stock cuts." They consisted of interchangeable designs—flags, knives, landscapes, etc.—inserted where specific details were unnecessary. The rule of thumb about the use of "stock cuts" as tail pieces in subscription was, if two-thirds of a page was empty the vacancy needed a picture. Bliss undoubtedly had hundreds of plates ready for such emergencies. Time schedules and troublesome illustrators—engravers as well as artists—were making *Roughing It* an emergency (Figs. 47, 48, & 49).

Figs. 47, 48, & 49. STOCK CUTS.

The need to fill white space makes suspect a number of other tail pieces in the book. Of the twenty-four inserted, four did not appear in the "List of Illustrations" and were probably last minute additions; two of these have Roberts and Richardson as engravers' signatures (the Roberts from page 118, Fig. 50, and Richardson from page 489); one has the unknown artist's signature P (page 390, Fig. 51); and the fourth one is the Chinese merchant from Knox. Many of the remaining fifteen suspicious prints were totally unrelated to the chapters and strongly resemble stock cuts.

Fig. 50. THE ENDOWMENT—TAIL-PIECE.

Fig. 51. WHERE IS THE RAM?—TAIL-PIECE.

Provable and probable borrowed prints begin to add up to significant numbers. The liberal borrowing from such varied sources suggests that Bliss was harried and therefore slipshod. Having finished canvassing available plates for his cuts he had to rush to compile a "List of Illustrations" which would include all the new engravings. This "List" was not up to Bliss's usual standards. *Roughing It* has, with the four above-cited tail pieces, 304 illustrations, not the 300 stated in most references. There were also two misplaced prints: illustration no. 126, CAMPING IN THE SNOW, cited as being on page 238, does not appear there but is inserted at the front of the book facing the frontispiece and the cut GREELEY'S RIDE, listed on page 150, is actually on page 151. Also, fourteen of the cuts have slightly different legends on the "List" than in the captions below the pictures.[43] There is no mention on the title page of specific illustrators, only a general statement: "FULLY ILLUSTRATED BY EMINENT ARTISTS."

During proofreading, Orion Clemens became suspicious of more than the previously mentioned inaccurate subject matter; he also began to suspect manipulation in illustrations and other money matters. He held off giving Twain information, however, until March 1872, when he (Orion) had left the employ of Bliss on the *American Publisher* and after the book's publication. Alerted about the problem, Twain wrote back to his brother:

> I cannot let you think that I overlook or underestimate the brotherly goodness & kindness of your motive in your assault upon Bliss. I would have you feel & know that I fully appreciate *that*, & value it. The fact that I condemn the *act* as being indefensible, does not in the least blind me to the virtue of the *motive* underlying it, or leave me unthankful for it. Livy & I have grieved sincerely over the thought of the depression & distress this matter is doubtless causing you. . . . There is no profit in remembering unpleasant things. Remember only that it has wrought one good: It has set you free from a humiliating servitude; a thing to be devoutly thankful for, God knows.[44]

His anger fuelled with Orion's suspicions, Mark Twain immediately rushed to a lawyer, who informed him that Bliss had violated a "verbal" rather than a written contractual agreement. Even if the "borrowing" could be proved, there was little to do legally. But Orion kept stoking his brother's mouldering fire with notes about the problem.

> Imagine the effect. . .on Bliss when he finds Hinckley [Bliss's bookkeeper] subpoenaed to testify as to borrowed engravings. . .; the testimony of the paper man as to its quality; of the Churchman pressman as to the country newspaper style of printing the cuts. . . . Bliss can see then that there is only needed to be added the testimony of some prominent engravers. . .to overwhelm with devastating ruin the subscription business and the American Publishing Company in particular.[45]

Orion probably had enough data to challenge Bliss. But Bliss's pirating of prints from books published by his own company could be considered a violation of the spirit, not the letter of the law. Whether the prints were owned by the artists, the engravers, or the American Publishing Company is a matter of legal opinion. Also, using stock cuts was admittedly a common practice in all publishing. If the editor-publisher did not add in the costs for these cuts it was considered ethical. If, however, the accounting ledgers listed artists' and engravers' fees for these same prints, that was another matter. Part of the Clemens brothers' objection was "based upon a claim by Bliss that the illustrations were new and more expensive than they actually were," rather than the legitimacy of his methods. Apparently Bliss had "used two sets of books. . ., one of which exaggerated the cost of paper, binding, and illustrating, and thus persuaded the author that there was a much smaller profit to divide."[46] The issue, however, was never fully explored, never taken to court, and never satisfactorily resolved. Distrust grew between Clemens and Bliss after publication of this book.

The first complete copies of *Roughing It* arrived from the bindery on 30 January 1872, almost two full months after the deposit of the title page. The book was a bulky, 591 page volume with 304 illustrations, meeting subscription standards in at least these two ways. The authorized English edition, like *The Innocents Abroad* before it, was issued, unillustrated, and in quite a different format.

The English edition, prepared in time for simultaneous publication to meet copyright law, was published in two volumes, *Roughing It* and *The Innocents at Home*. It omitted the three appendices to the American edition but included *Mark Twain's (Burlesque) Autobiography.*[47]

This edition bore the entire burden of Bliss's problems with illustration. Illustrated page proofs had not been sent to Routledge in England because of the long delays. To make sure of publishing concurrently for secure copyright, Routledge issued a cheaply manufactured set of two volumes in yellow board covers with illustrations only on the front cover.[48] Despite the fact that there were no prints, the books retained Twain's directed reference to both Senator Stewart's portrait and the Chinese wash bill. These problems of illustrated copy and copyright would take much of Twain's time when he came to the publication of *The Gilded Age* and *The Adventures of Tom Sawyer.*

During the first three months after publication the sales of *Roughing It* were promising. But by the end of the year sales

had plummeted to about a thousand copies a month, the total
for the first two years was a disappointing 73, 207. The English
edition also sold fewer copies than had *The Innocents Abroad.*
   Clemens blamed everything on Bliss and the company:

> So Roughing It sells less than twice as many in a quarter
> as Innocents, a book which is getting gray with age.
> The fault is mainly in the engravings and paper, I think.—
> That, and the original lack of publicity.[49]

Bliss was responsible for the poor manufacture and the scarce
publicity, but he couldn't be blamed for the unfavorable reviews.

   Howells, so flattering in his critique of *The Innocents
Abroad*, was slightly less impressed this time, labelling Mark
Twain's work a "grotesque exaggeration" and in another paragraph remarking on the "thousand anecdotes, relevant and
irrelevant, [that] embroider the work; excursions and digres-
sions of all kinds are the very woof of it." He continued, "it is
not unbrokenly nor infallibly funny; nor is it to be always
praised for all the literary virtues; but it is singularly entertaining, . . . amiable, manly, and generous."[50]   Charitably, he
made no comment on the illustrations. Twain was generally
pleased with the review.

   The *Overland Monthly*, however, did comment on design:

> Of the three hundred wood-cuts that illustrate the volume
> we can say nothing complimentary, from an artistic point
> of view.   But some of them are spirited, and many of
> them suggestive. Crude as they are in design, and coarse
> in execution, they have afforded us much amusement; and
> the majority of readers would, we are sure, regret to dis-
> pense with them.[51]

   The book had been a cut-and-paste operation.   Mark
Twain's inconsistent text got little support from the inferior and
unsympathetic sketches, the cheap paper, and the poor quality of
printing. *Roughing It* was the culmination of eighteen months of
delayed manuscript, constant revising of text and illustrations, a
chaotic method of design and engraving processes, and the
pressure of publishing deadlines.   The combination of Elisha
Bliss, Williams and friends, and Mark Twain proved unsuccessful

both artistically and financially. Twain had learned costly lessons: he would have to do more than compile random stories; he would have to try to link narrative and illustration; and, to this end, he would have to become involved in the business and production end of his next book, *The Gilded Age.*

Notes

[1] "Contract for *Roughing It*," [15 July 1870] *Mark Twain Quarterly*, 6, no. 3 (Summer/Fall 1944), 5.

[2] SLC to Mrs. Fairbanks, 29 May [1870], *MTMF*, p. 131.

[3] SLC to Orion Clemens, 8 April [1871], *MTLP*, p. 63.

[4] *MTB*, I, 438.

[5] SLC to EB, 2 August 1870, *MTLP*, p. 37. In the next line of this letter Clemens reminds Bliss again of a portrait for *Roughing It*: "Yes, we'll put the portrait in the new book."

[6] SLC to EB, 3 May [1871], *MTLP*, p. 66.

[7] SLC to EB, 15 May 1871, *MTL*, 188.

[8] SLC to EB, 22 December 1870, *ET&S*, 1, 572-573. In SLC to EB, 5 January 1871, Clemens again suggested Mullen as an illustrator: "The curious beasts & great contrasts in this Pre-deluge article offer a gorgeous chance for the artist's fancy & ingenuity, I think. Send both sketches to Mullen—he is the man to do them, I guess" (*ET&S*, 1, 574). This postscript alludes to an extract from Mark Twain's long-germinating "Noah's Ark book" which was never published.

[9] Orion Clemens to SLC, 25 January 1871, MTP. Published in part in *ET&S*, 1, 584.

[10] Mullen's signed prints appear on pages 268, 301, 482 (AN ENEMY'S PRAYER), and 488 of the first American edition. Most cuts in Chapters LXVII and LXVIII are also in his style.

[11] EB to SLC, 17 May 1871, *MTLP*, p. 66, note 5.

[12] EB to SLC, 7 July 1871, *MTLP*, p. 68, note 1.

[13] *MT&EB*, p. 57. "It was Bliss who had given the new book the title of *Roughing It*. *Innocents at Home* had been its provisional title, certainly a misleading one, though it has been retained in England for the second volume" (*MTB*, I, 452, note 1). "Clemens later recalled Bliss's role in

naming the book. 'Oh, that is the last thing to be thought about. I never write a title until I finish a book,' he told a reporter, 'and then I frequently don't know what to call it. I usually write out anywhere from a half dozen to two dozen and a half titles, and the publisher casts his experienced eye over them and guides me largely in the selection. That's what I did in the case of *Roughing It*, and, in fact, it has always been my practice' " (Interview in the St. Louis *Post Dispatch*, 12 May 1882, reprinted in Louis Budd's "Interviews with Samuel L. Clemens, 1874-1910," *American Literary Realism* [Winter 1977], pp. 37-39).

[14] SLC to Olivia, 27 November 1871, *The Love Letters of Mark Twain*, ed. Dixon Wecter (New York: Harper and Brothers, 1949), p. 166. SEVERE CASE OF STAGE-FRIGHT appears on page 561 of the first edition.

[15] Notes on an early lecture in Fig. 3 show borrowings from many stories and is preserved in the Copley Library, La Jolla, California. The lecture notes in Fig. 4, relating specifically to *Roughing It*, were preserved by Isabel Lyon, personal secretary to Samuel Clemens. In her notebooks she remarks:

> This [Fig. 4] Mark Twain sketch for lecture notes is extremely important. It shows his habit of using such notes; notes, obscure to another as he intended them to be; but to him, clear & stimulating. . . . Lecturing had become a sore trial to him. . .the folding of it [the note] indicates that it had been carried in Mr. Clemens' seat pocket (a habit of his), during the lecture period, for he would give the same one [lecture] many times if it were talking well. And this was a great success for he was using parts of "Roughing It."

According to Isabel Lyon the lecture notes were handed to Charles Stoddard, a poet and writer friend of Clemens in the early California days, who happened to be in London in 1873 acting as Clemens' secretary. This transaction occurred at the final Liverpool lecture at the close of the English season of 1873-4. The notes in the margins on Fig. 4 were ultimately deciphered by W. L. Brown of the Associated Press, who knew the Mark Twain West. A copy of the sketch is in the McKinney Papers file (Isabel Lyon to Mr. Howe, 26 March 1938, Jean Webster McKinney Family Papers, Vassar College Library, File 1938).

[16] Orion to SLC, 4 July 1871, *MT&EB*, pp. 57-58. The pictures of Carson City, circa 1861, in the Mark Twain Papers show a generous growth of trees even though Clemens chose not to acknowledge them in his text.

[17] Mark Twain, *Roughing It* (Hartford: American Publishing Company,

1872), p. 157. Hereafter cited as *Roughing It,* 1872.
    [18]*Roughing It,* 1872, p. 178. Print appears on page 179 of the first edition.
    [19]*Roughing It,* 1872, p. 181. Print, captioned UNIVERSALLY UN-SETTLED, appears on the same page, 181, of the first edition.
    [20]*Roughing It,* 1872, p. 182. Print, captioned RIDING THE PLUG, appears on the same page of the first edition.
    [21]The tail piece appears captioned THE CHURCH-GOING BELL in Albert Richardson's *Beyond the Mississippi* (Hartford: American Publishing Company, 1867), p. 216 and in *Roughing It,* 1872, p. 489.
    [22]Paine's comment on original letter: "The letter is in Mr. Greeley's characteristic scrawl, and no doubt furnished inspiration for the turnip story in *Roughing It,* also the model for the pretended facsimile of Greeley's writing" (*MTB,* I, 438). Print of original letter from Horace Greeley to Mark Twain is reproduced on page 439 of *MTB.* Greeley's letter is the only illustration reproduced in the text for the authoritative *The Works of Mark Twain: Roughing It,* ed. Franklin Rogers and Paul Baender (Berkeley, Los Angeles, and London: University of California Press, 1972). Hereafter cited as *Works: Roughing It.* In notes for this edition the editors explain: "The first-edition illustration is reproduced because of its importance to the chapter" (p. 639, note 453). The print of Horace Greeley's letter appears on page 509 of the first edition of *Roughing It.* Coincidentally, a FACSIMILE OF HORACE GREELEY'S MANUSCRIPT (from a TRIBUNE EDITORIAL, 1866) appears in Richardson's *Beyond the Mississippi,* p. 164 and the reproduction in *Roughing It* resembles it.
    [23]The caricatures appear in the first edition on the following pages: Horace Greeley, p. 151; Calvin Higbie, p. 282; Dan De Quille, p. 362. Though Dan De Quille is not referred to as specifically as the others in the book, it is known that Dan was "twice confined for 'delerium tremens' during 1869 and was discharged from the Territorial Enterprise in 1870, and apparently not for the first time, for drunkenness" (*The Journals of Alfred Doten:* 1849-1903, 2: 10771-11119). The likeness and the textual reference to "intemperate habits" make Dan De Quille a likely model for the cut.
    [24]SLC to "Dear Br.", 18 [July] 1870, *CL2.* Also see note 59, Chapter I.
    [25]Senator William M. Stewart of Nevada. Mark Twain was his private secretary briefly in 1867. When Stewart wrote his memoirs, according to Milton Meltzer, the Senator "did not remember Mark fondly" (*MTHim,* p. 104). There is, apparently, no extant comment from Mark Twain on why *Roughing It,* 1872 contains no recognizable likeness of Senator Stewart.

²⁶*Roughing It,* 1872, p. 309.

²⁷*Roughing It,* 1872, p. 309. "TRY A FEW?" appears on page 309; the "portrait" appears on page 310 of the first edition.

²⁸An "S" on the cut suggests that Roswell Shurtleff may have been the illustrator for this print.

²⁹William Morris Stewart, *Reminiscences of Senator William M. Stewart* (New York: Neale Publishing Company, 1908), pp. 219-224. "William M. Stewart was United States Senator for Nevada from 1864 to 1875 and also from 1887 to 1905. . . . In Nevada he was the most prominent lawyer of the state, a member of the Territorial Council in 1861 and a delegate to the Constitutional Convention of 1863. In late 1867 and early 1868 Clemens roomed in the same house in Washington and served as his private secretary. The two men quarreled before Clemens left Washington. The comment here and an accompanying 'portrait' in the first edition may be echoes of this rupture" *(Works: Roughing It,* 1972, pp. 584-585, Item 279.35).

³⁰"Full-page illustrations facing the frontispiece and that facing p. 100 are both signed 'Shurtleff,' others signed 'S' or 'R. S.' [pp. 246, 294, 297, 310, 321, and 362] may also be his, as may some others [pp. 353, 355, 384, 386, 387, 388, 567, and 569] signed with a monogram which could be either 'R. S.' or 'S. R.' " (Hamilton, I: 207). "Some of the illustrations are after drawings by R. M. Shurtleff" (Hamilton, I: 224).

³¹EB to SLC, 6 December 1871, *MT&EB,* p. 58.

³²Cuts with suspicious markings: Roberts, p. 118; Lauderback, p. 535; Langridge, p. 147; and Richardson (the Stephens drawings) on pp. 183 and 489 of the first edition, cited in Hamilton, I: 224. References to each of the engravers are included in the following source: "William E. Roberts, wood engraver, active in NYC from 1846 to 1876" *(The New York Historical Society's Dictionary of Artists in America: 1564-1860,* ed. George C. Groce and David H. Wallace (New Haven: Yale University Press, 1957), p. 540). Lauderback of Lauderback and Hoffman, "Wood engravers and designers, Philadelphia, 1853-1869" (Groce, p. 404). "Richardson, James (1848-1880), wood engraver of the firms Orr and Richardson (1848) and Richardson and Cox (1853-59)" (Groce, p. 536).

³³Some 53 of the 300 illustrations "bear the name or initials of Williams" (Hamilton, I: 224). The Warren cut in *Roughing It* appears on page 254 of the first edition and is on page 502 of *Beyond the Mississippi.* The markings T. M. and P occur respectively on page 542 and page 390 of the first edition.

³⁴*MT&EB,* p. 194, note 110. Professor Hill located many of these prints from the Knox and Richardson books. My research has located the prints in J. Ross Browne, the borrowing of "Emperor of Russia," page 393

in *The Innocents Abroad,* page 400 in Knox; and "Queen of Greece," page 355 in *The Innocents Abroad,* page 397 in Knox. For further work in this area of print-borrowing, see Beverly R. David, "Those Pirated Prints: Illustrating Mark Twain's *Roughing It,*" *Mark Twain Journal,* XX (Winter 1979-1980), 1-5.

[35]SLC to "Dear Bro.", 18 April [1871], *MTLP,* p. 54.

[36]"You want to know something about the route between California and Nevada territory?. . .take a winter view, J. Ross Brown's [sic] picture, in *Harper's Monthly,*" SLC to Jane Clemens and Pamela Moffett, 8-9 February 1862, *CL*1. "I [Clemens] lectured in Oakland the other night,— guest of J. Ross Browne & his charming family," SLC to Jane Clemens, 5 December 1866, *CL*1.

[37]Duncan Emrick, *Comstock Bonanza* (New York: Vanguard Press, Inc., 1950), p. 5; *Adventures in the Apache Country,* ed. Donald M. Powell (Tuscon: University of Arizona Press, 1974), xiii; Walter Blair, *Native American Humor* (New York; American Book Company, 1937), pp. xix-xx; *J. Ross Browne, His Letters, and Writings,* ed. Linda Ferguson Browne (Albuquerque: University of New Mexico Press, 1969), pp. xii-xx.

[38]Location of prints: *J. Ross Browne, Adventures in the Apache Country* (New York: Harper and Brothers, 1869), pages 532, 438, 289, 408, and 500. Corresponding prints in *Roughing It,* 1872, are on pages 253, facing 265, 260, 302, and 340.

[39]Location of altered prints: Albert Richardson, *Beyond the Mississippi* (Hartford: American Publishing Company, 1867), p. 295, captioned OUR HOUSE IN DENVER; p. 279, THE AUTHOR ARRIVES IN DENVER; p. 487, TAIL-PIECE [Murderer]. Corresponding in *Roughing It,* 1872, p. 50, PRAIRIE DOGS; p. 323, MAGNIFICENCE AND MISERY; p. 557, TAIL-PIECE [Liar].

[40]*Roughing It,* 1872, p. 392. This cut appears on page 392 of the first edition of *Roughing It* and on page 436 of *Beyond the Mississippi.*

[41]Thomas Knox, *Overland Through Asia* (Hartford: American Publishing Company, 1870), p. 338.

[42]*Roughing It,* 1872, p. 395.

[43]According to Merle Johnson, "It is interesting to note, but of no value in determining the actual first state of this book, that illustration No. 126 listed as being at page 238 does not actually appear there but is inserted at the front of the book. The plate, *Camping in the Snow,* appears in this position in all copies of the first and subsequent editions that I have examined. Also, illustration No. 92 is listed as *Fight at Lake Tahoe;* the plate itself is correctly captioned *Fire at Lake Tahoe*" (*BMT,* p. 14).

Variations in captioning: (1) "List of Illustrations," (2) caption below inserted print.

	No.	Caption	Page
(1)	48	THE PARTED STREAMS.	101
(2)		THE PARTED STREAM.	
(1)	92	FIGHT AT LAKE TAHOE (FULL PAGE).	176 Face
(2)		FIRE AT LAKE TAHOE.	Page
(1)	100	SATISFACTORY VOUCHERS.	190
(2)		SATISFACTORY VOUCHER.	
(1)	151	THE COMPROMISE.	290
(2)		ENFORCING A COMPROMISE.	
(1)	160	BIRDS EYE VIEW OF VIRGINIA CITY AND MT. DAVIDSON.	304
(2)		BIRD'S EYE VIEW OF VIRGINIA AND MOUNT DAVIDSON.	
(1)	173	SCOTTY BRIGGS AND THE MINISTER.	331
(2)		COMMITTEEMAN AND MINISTER.	
(1)	176	SCOTTY AS S.S. TEACHER.	338
(2)		SCOTTY AS A SUNDAY-SCHOOL TEACHER.	
(1)	177	THE MAN WHO HAD KILLED HIS DOZEN.	340
(2)		THE MAN WHO HAD KILLED A DOZEN.	
(1)	188	THERE SAT THE LAWYER.	365
(2)		UNLOOKED-FOR APPEARANCE OF THE LAWYER.	
(1)	214	A NEW ENGLAND SCENE.	409
(2)		AN EASTERN LANDSCAPE.	
(1)	248	SIT DOWN TO LISTEN.	467
(2)		SAT DOWN TO LISTEN.	
(1)	275	BREAKING THE TABU.	521
(2)		THE TABU BROKEN.	

(1)	276	SURF BATHING.	525
(2)		SURF-BATHING—SUCCESS.	
(1)	283	BROKE THROUGH.	539
(2)		BREAKING THROUGH.	
(1)	299	THE BEST OF THE JOKE.	569
(2)		BEST PART OF THE JOKE.	

[44]SLC to "My dear Bro," 7 March 1872, *CL* 3. An editor's note to this letter claims that Orion Clemens parted company with Bliss and the *American Publisher*, which would list him as editor for the last time in April 1872. The final cause of Orion's departure was his claim that his brother was being defrauded on production costs for *Roughing It*. Correspondence from Orion which may have precipitated this consoling response is not extant, but a letter of 17 May 1872 indicates that he felt his brother could successfully seek a court ruling against Bliss on grounds of "borrowed engravings."

[45]Hamlin Hill, "Mark Twain's Quarrels with Elisha Bliss," *American Literature*, XXXIII, No. 4 (January 1962), 446. Also in *MT&EB*, p. 66.

[46]*MT&EB*, p. 67.

[47]*MTinEng*, p. 32.

[48]*Works: Roughing It*, pp. 21-22.

[49]*MTLP*, p. 74.

[50]*MTCH*, 48-49. The original, William Dean Howells: unsigned review, *Atlantic Monthly* (June 1872), pp. 754-755.

[51]*MTCH*, p. 51. Originally, unsigned review, *Overland Monthly* (June 1872), pp. 580-581.

List of Illustrations: *Roughing It*

Chapter IV

The Gilded Age: A Tale of To-day

"They have . . . laid violent hands upon well-known public men."
New York *World* ("Notices of the Press," 1873)

After the publication of *Roughing It*, Mark Twain began to re-evaluate his position as an author of subscription books. The swirling criticisms about inferior quality in drawings, paper, and printing had shaken his faith in Bliss while thoughts of preparing another massive manuscript made the other, less demanding publishing markets look very inviting. Probably another motive— a more subtle one—resulted from his move into the fashionable writers' haven of Nook Farm. Consorting with the local *literati* had Twain fantasizing about being accepted as a man of letters rather than just the community's literary humorist.

A plan for a collaborative writing venture with his new friend and neighbor, Charles Dudley Warner, seemed a happy solution. Together they decided to write a semi-fictional political book burlesquing the then fast-selling "sensation" novel. A novel, not being the usual stuff of the subscription traffic, gave the pair reason to approach Sheldon and Company, the trade firm that had produced *(Burlesque) Autobiography*. Clemens rationalized that Sheldon would be less devious and more malleable than publisher Elisha Bliss. Indeed, at this date, Clemens regarded Sheldon as a humanitarian anxious to treat an author generously; someone with a mind open to unique ideas of style and design. As it turned out, talks with Sheldon served only as a device for maneuvering a more lucrative contract from Bliss.

While working on the manuscript Clemens' conscience nagged him into acknowledging to Bliss the possibly of his publishing in an alternate market. He hesitatingly explained in a letter: "We [Twain and Warner] shall doubtless be ready to talk business by about Tuesday. . . . Sheldon & Co. think we will make a serious and damaging mistake if we try to sell a novel by subscription."[1] Bliss, catching the hint and fearful of losing one of his current best-selling authors, quickly responded. He assured both writers that the promotional schemes used for selling sub-scription travel books would work as effectively for a novel. Bliss also sweetened the deal: he raised Clemens' usual seven and a half percent royalty to ten percent (five percent for each author), offered a written guarantee of excellence in design (to offset Clemens' unhappiness about *Roughing It*), and inserted a line in the contract giving the authors supervision over the illus-trations:

> The book is to be after the style of "The Innocents Abroad" & equal it in quality—of its paper binding, engravings, & printing—. The engravings inserted to be mutually acceptable.[2]

This contract would seem to avoid some of the problems associated with the earlier book and also provide another golden opportunity for large profits. Clemens and Warner signed with Bliss for the publication of *The Gilded Age.*

Having chosen to stay in the subscription field, Clemens re-solved to become more involved in the business end of the company. Control over the physical aspects of the published book was only a first step; Clemens also wanted access to the firm's financial statements, as well as a seat on the board. He had already invested money in the company and now requested "as soon as I can get some more stock at easy figures, I want it. I want to be a Director, also."[3] Clemens became a Director in 1873, before the publication of *The Gilded Age,* and remained on the board until 1881.

Meanwhile, even before writing manuscript, Mark Twain had formulated his own concepts for the book. He had told William Dean Howells that Warner would work up the fiction and he would "hurl in the facts." Twain's inspiration for these facts came from several sources: stories about and the history of his own family joined to journalistic writings and cartoons in con-temporary newspapers and magazines. Twain's plan was to couple the eccentricities of his relatives with current accounts of political corruption in Washington and New York. For added spice he would blend in the details of a scandal-filled murder trial in San Francisco. The newspapers had plenty of grist for his writer's mill. In eastern politics the Greeley-Grant presidential campaign had challenged the last vestiges of Tammany Hall; the

Credit-Mobilier bribery ruckus had ruined Congressmen Oakes Ames and James Brooks; and proof of malfeasance in Senator Pomeroy's Congressional vote had reached its inevitable denouement on the floor of the Kansas State House. On the opposite coast, the tabloids' headlines were debating the merits and demerits of the jury system in the lurid and grisly trial of Laura Fair in the state of California.[4]

Mark Twain's facts about Pomeroy and Fair, who became Dilworthy and Hawkins in *The Gilded Age,* were largely derived from his reading of the illustrated news. Twain paraphrased the political demise of Pomeroy/Dilworthy directly from editorials in *Harper's Weekly* illustrated with cartoons and accurate renderings of the proceedings by on-the-spot artists. Similarly, Twain's narrative of the Laura Hawkins trial was based on the accounts of the West coast Fair trial from pages complete with portraits of the "temporarily insane" murderess. Since Mark Twain's manuscript scrupulously followed the printed versions of both stories (at times word-for-word), it was only natural for him to want to have creditable artists copy the newspapers' pictures and cartoons as engravings for the book.

The logical artist for this kind of muckraking was, of course, Thomas Nast. As the most important cartoonist of the time, he daily harassed the counterparts of Twain-Warner's semifictional characters in his *Harper's* cartoons (Fig. 1). Nast was first in Twain's mind. The author envisioned combining his own and Warner's story-telling talents with the visual skills of Nast to produce a block-busting *roman à clef.* He broached the idea to Bliss in a letter written early in 1873:

> Now Nast appears to be doing nothing in particular. I want him, solitary & alone, to illustrate this next book [*The Gilded Age*], it being an essentially *American* book, he will enjoy doing it. Nast only has just one *first-class* talent (caricature), & no more—but this book will exercise that talent, I think. I think he will be glad to do this work below his usual terms. If you say so *I will write him.* Tell me what you think, & tell me about the total amount you think it best to put in the *drawing* of the illustrations.[5]

For the first time, Clemens was spelling out to Bliss ideas and specific conditions for illustrating his book and these were more than mere suggestions. Clemens had learned with *Roughing It* that a set contract fee for one artist would help prevent a recurrence of Bliss's double bookkeeping for engravings. It would also insure some consistency in the prints—a feature sadly lacking in all of Mark Twain's earlier publications. As important as cost and consistency were to Twain, his main concern was to have the drawings done by a gifted caricaturist, since he deemed caricature to be a critical design concept for the book.

Clemens' proposal of a Warner-Twain-Nast publishing combination was no idle expectation. At least two of the three men, Twain and Nast, had often talked of a team effort. Back in 1867, Nast had suggested a "collaborative lecture tour; Clemens to lecture and Nast to illuminate the remarks with his swift brilliant caricatures."[6]   Unfortunately, conflicting work schedules (Twain was preparing to sail on the *Quaker City*) had made the tour impossible. Ten years later Clemens proposed the same kind of scheme to Nast. This time, the late seventies, Nast was both too ill and too busy to consider an extended tour. The traveling chalk talks were never realized.

The two men did manage to combine talents in two minor publications. A year before he moved to Hartford, Mark Twain had submitted four short stories to Nast's *Almanac*. Nast accepted two of the four: "The Late Ben Franklin" and "The Story of The Good Little Boy Who Did Not Prosper." They saw print in the 1872 and 1873 editions respectively with characteristic Nast cartoons (Fig. 2). In a letter Nast hinted to Twain: "A good many of your other things too, ought to be illustrated. How does the idea strike you and upon what terms would you go into such a speculation."[7]   Twain replied that the idea was splendid and asked if the cartoonist could accompany him to England where they could design an English travel book. In a letter he wrote his wish: "I do hope my publishers can make it pay you to illustrate my English book. Then I should have good pictures. They've got to improve on 'Roughing It' "[8] Apologetically Nast declined, again incapacitated by illness—a chronic case of catarrh. Realistically, with his declining health, the artist needed to continue his profitable newspaper work in order to support his large family. For Nast it would have been financial suicide to tackle a time-consuming book that would take him out of the country. Therefore, despite their obvious rapport and their desire to combine skills, lack of time and money frustrated all such plans.

THOMAS NAST, THE ECONOMICAL COUNCIL, ALBANY,
NEW YORK.
Fig. 1.

22   *NAST'S ALMANAC FOR* 1873

THE STORY OF THE GOOD LITTLE BOY WHO DID NOT PROSPER.

BY MARK TWAIN.

ONCE there was a good little boy by the name of Jacob Blivens. He always obeyed his parents, no matter how absurd and unreasonable their demands were; and he always learned his book, and never was late at Sabbath-school. He would not play hookey, even when his sober judgment told him it was the most profitable thing he could do. None of the other boys could ever make that boy out, he acted so strangely. He wouldn't lie, no matter how convenient it was. He just said it was wrong to lie, and that was sufficient for him. And he was so honest that he was simply ridiculous. The curious ways that Jacob had surpassed every thing. He wouldn't play at marbles on Sunday, he wouldn't rob birds' nests, he wouldn't give hot pennies to organ-grinders' monkeys; he didn't seem to take any interest in any kind of rational amusement. So the other boys used to try to reason it out, and come to an understanding of him, but they couldn't arrive at any satisfactory conclusion; as I said

Fig. 2. NAST'S ALAMANAC FOR 1873.

Unfortunately, Clemens' latest proposal to Bliss about Nast as an illustrator for *The Gilded Age* had no resolution, for reasons now unknown. Bliss quickly contacted another illustrator, William T. Smedley, whose star was rising. At the time Smedley was working for *Harper's Weekly* and was a close friend of William Dean Howells, who may have suggested his name to Clemens or Bliss. Smedley must have actively considered the commission, for Bliss immediately forwarded manuscript to him so that he could work on designs. Smedley, however, was not hired, either because he was too expensive or because he could not come up to the critical standards of authors and editor. Bliss did pay him for one full-page drawing captioned A SPRAY OF BOX, though it was never used. It was meant to illustrate a conversation between Laura and Mr. Buckstone, one of her admirers, concerning a forgotten floral remembrance recounted in Chapter XXXVII.[9] Another cut, captioned PLAYING TO WIN, eventually illustrated the scene and filled the allotted space in the first edition (Fig. 3).

PLAYING TO WIN.

Fig. 3. PLAYING TO WIN.

Examining the list of acceptable illustrators, all parties finally agreed on a third possiblity, Augustus Hoppin. Hoppin had been a long-time practitioner in the illustrating field, his work appearing in magazines in the late forties and in book illustration in the early fifties. His specialty was an amiable satirizing of polite society. The critics often called him an American Du Maurier, although the parallel was mostly a jingoistic exaggeration.[10] The English Du Maurier's cartoons on the continent perhaps equalled Nast's in the States, but Hoppin's did not. He was fashionable rather than caustic and certainly not in the same class with Nast, Du Maurier, or Smedley.

Nevertheless, Clemens approved of Hoppin and appreciated that his talent would be sufficient to successfully caricature the figures in the novel. A more prudent argument also probably prevailed for the final decision. With Nast and Smedley crossed off the list, the authors were short of both time and candidates. Hoppin proved the acceptable alternative.

The fact is that both Olivia and Samuel Clemens knew and may have been favorably swayed to Hoppin as illustrator for the new work. A copy of Howells' latest book with drawings by Hoppin, *Their Wedding Journey*, had been sent to the couple by Howells and, according to written testimony, it quickly became one of the most prized volumes in their library. Shortly thereafter, Olivia, especially pleased with the book's design, bought a rather expensive edition of *Ups and Downs on Land and Water*, a book written and illustrated by the same Hoppin.[11]

The hiring of Hoppin caused everyone to take a second look at the budget. Loaded with commissions, Hoppin undoubtedly commanded a substantial fee—presumably lower than Nast but certainly higher than True Williams or Will Smedley. Commissioning three hundred or more drawings from a high-priced artist would prove very expensive. Bliss and the authors compromised: Hoppin would do only important full-page prints. Less costly artists would be hired to make the smaller cuts. Though this would inevitably lead again to inconsistency in illustration and characterization, financial prudence won out over aesthetic standards.

The obvious choice for sketching the small inserted cuts was the American Publishing Company's perennial workhorse, True Williams. As it turned out, Williams even contributed three full-page prints along with at least twenty-five smaller inserts—all twenty-eight cuts signed.[12]   Taking no chances that the tippling Williams might again prove unreliable, Bliss also hired (rather than this time surreptitiously appropriating the work of) several other artists who had worked for the company before.

Henry Louis Stephens would finally appear "officially" as an illustrator of a major Mark Twain work with credit given on the title page of the firm's edition. Stephens had, of course, been commissioned by Bliss for Richardson's *Beyond the Mississippi*, thereby unofficially contributing two drawings to *Roughing It* through Bliss's controversial pirating of prints. Stephens' primary skill was as a caricaturist/cartoonist, having drawn for

Frank Leslie's illustrated news in the fifties, the comic paper *Vanity Fair* in the sixties, and *Punchinello*, a short-lived comic weekly, in the late sixties.

Clemens may have been instrumental in hiring Stephens. He could have argued persuasively that his work on *(Burlesque) Autobiography* had superbly captured the features of everyone from Fisk to Tweed. With Hoppin working caricature into the full-page prints, Stephens had the ability to do the same for the inserted cuts. Unfortunately, Stephens' facility for fine caricature would appear in very few of the final drawings. It is impossible, however, to say precisely which or how many drawings were done by Stephens, since only prints by Hoppin and Williams were signed.[13]

The title page of the first edition read: "FULLY ILLUS-TRATED FROM NEW DESIGNS by Hoppin, Stephens, Williams, White, Etc., Etc." A most curious addition to this list is the name of George G. White. White and Stephens had been a collaborative team on a number of books in the late sixties, most notably Whitehead's *The New House That Jack Built*, which may have inspired ideas for the cartoons in Mark Twain's ill-fated *(Burlesque) Autobiography*. White had also worked for Bliss on *Beyond the Mississippi*, drawing twenty illustrations. Curiously, there is only one certifiable White print in *The Gilded Age*, an uncaptioned tail piece for Chapter XVII. This identical cut, captioned THE CITY OF NEW BABYLON IN FACT, also had been inserted as a small print in *Beyond the Mississippi* (Figs. 4 & 5).

White's credit as an illustrator for this Mark Twain work has confused bibliographers for decades.[14] This acknowledged White print does prove that the pirating of prints remained an unshakable habit for Bliss. To his credit, however, the only samples of pilferage in *The Gilded Age* were the above Babylonian scene and several stock pieces—for example, the often-used snake entwined about its prey (Fig. 6).

The fact that all the candidates for principal illustrators—Nast, Smedley, Hoppin, and Stephens—were well-known caricaturists indicates that all parties saw caricature as one of the major concepts for illustrating *The Gilded Age*. An examination of the first edition reveals what the illustrators contributed—or failed to contribute—toward the realization of this concept.

Augustus Hoppin, as featured artist, drew sixteen full-page prints, inking his broadly scripted "Hoppin" prominently into the corner of each one. Neither his characteristic style nor his signature is detectable in other full-page or inserted cuts. His prints featured the primary characters: Laura, Ruth, Sellers,

Fig. 4. TAIL PIECE.

THE CITY OF NEW BABYLON IN FACT.

Fig. 5. THE CITY OF NEW BABYLON IN FACT.

Fig. 6. TAIL PIECE.

LAURA'S VISIT TO THE BOOK STORE

Fig. 7. LAURA'S VISIT TO THE BOOKSTORE.

and Washington. His flair for fashion was especially notable in the drawings of the women. Laura appears to step directly from the contemporary society pages, with stylish trends meticulously copied, even to the fine details of ribboned bows and bouffant bustles (Fig. 7). But it was not merely in his feeling for style or fashion that Hoppin was up to date. In two specific prints, SENATOR DILLWORTHY [sic] ADDRESSING THE SUNDAY SCHOOL and LAURA RECEIVES DILLWORTHY'S [sic] BLESSING (curiously both incorrectly spelled in the captions, though not in the "List of Illustrations"), Hoppin used the features of a contemporary politician, Senator Pomeroy, as his model (Figs. 8, 9, & 10).

An important part of Mark Twain's narrative centers on a Senator Abner Dilworthy who had been caught buying votes for his re-election and had been subsequently cleared of the charge in a Senate investigation. In the early outline for the novel, Twain had boldly called his senator "Bumroy," a barely disguised, witty substitute for Pomeroy, the name of the guilty senator in real life. Senator Samuel Clarke Pomeroy's vote-purchasing deals had hit the pages of the newspapers in January, February, and March of 1873, at the same time Mark Twain was writing his novel. Hoppin, acting on his own or with suggestions, had accurately copied Pomeroy for his Dilworthy illustrations. Dilworthy was presented in a dozen full-page and inserted cuts: two executed by Hoppin and a number by Williams—two signed "TW" and others that match his style. Twain's anecdote coupled with the Hoppin-Williams identifiable caricatures gave the readers both pictorial and written evidence for linking the fictional to the real politician.[15]

Still another visual parallel to a living congressman was successfully rendered by the illustrators, enabling *The Gilded Age* really to live up to its sub-title, *A Tale of To-day*. This second identifiable personality was Senator James Nye of Nevada, whom Twain caricatured as Senator Balloon. Mark Twain had in his manuscript notes come tantalizingly close to identifying his real-life character by naming him Bly. He later, as he had with Bumroy-Dilworthy, substituted the name "Balloon," somewhat obscuring the identity. When Twain wrote of Balloon's antics, however, he faithfully reproduced in every detail one of Nye's most publicized escapades: his abuse of the Congressional franking privilege, a small fraud which finally cost him his Senate seat. According to Twain's text:

SENATOR DILLWORTHY ADDRESSING THE SUNDAY SCHOOL.

SENATOR DILLWORTHY [sic] ADDRESSING THE SUNDAY
SCHOOL.
Fig. 8.

LAURA RECEIVES DILLWORTHY'S BLESSING.

LAURA RECEIVES DILLWORTHY'S [sic] BLESSING.
Fig. 9.

HON. SAMUEL C. POMEROY, UNITED STATES SENATOR FROM KANSAS.
[FROM A PHOTOGRAPH BY BRADY, OF WASHINGTON.]

HON. SAMUEL C. POMEROY, UNITED STATES SENATOR FROM KANSAS.
Fig. 10.

"ALL CONGRESSMEN DO THAT."

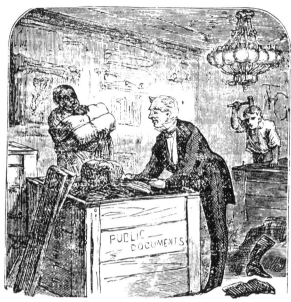

Fig. 11. "ALL CONGRESSMEN DO THAT."

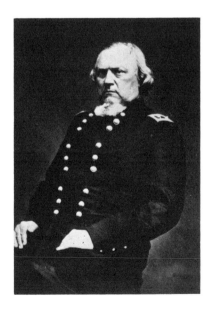

JAMES W. NYE. TERRITORIAL GOVERNOR AND UNITED STATES SENATOR, NEVADA.
Fig. 12.

> Senator Balloon put fifteen cents worth of stamps on each of those seven huge boxes of old clothes, and shipped that ton of second-hand rubbish, old boots and pantaloons and what not through the mails as registered matter![16]

Mark Twain's narration of the humorous shipping incident and the illustrator's use of Nye's features on the figure stuffing the packing crates in two of the cuts make the resemblance between Nye and Balloon unmistakable. Although the Balloon illustrations are not as skillfully executed as the Dilworthy, Twain's readers had as little trouble matching Nye to Balloon as they did Dilworthy to Pomeroy (Figs. 11 & 12).

It seems that Mark Twain understood Nye as a "seasoned" politician. Both Twain and his brother had known Nye when the latter was the Territorial Governor of Nevada and had followed his career when he went into the U. S. Senate. Twain had considered him an expert liar and had frequently lampooned him in the news dispatches he wrote for the *Territorial Enterprise.*[17] It is now impossible to ascertain whether credit for the Balloon-Nye look-alikes should go to Stephens, with his proven ability in caricature, or to Williams—who, one gathers from some of his signed sketches, was doing on-the-job training in this new technique. Nor is there any evidence to prove whether Mark Twain made suggestions on the matter to either artist.

Other visual parallels, though identifiable, seem to be only half-hearted attempts at caricature. Mr. Buckstone, Chairman of the House Committee on Benevolent Appropriation and later Laura's suitor, has the Roman nose and pouting mouth of his real counterpart, Ralph Buckland, though he here appears more angular (Figs. 13 & 14). The Buckstone of Figure 13, however, was certainly inconsistent with the Buckstone sketched in the previously discussed PLAYING TO WIN cut of an earlier chapter. Luckily Mark Twain retained the "Buck" in the surname to conveniently cement the identity for the reader. The artist's Indian-swindling Brother Balaam admittedly has the bushy eyebrows, penetrating stare, and patrician nose (though not the beard) of his double, the Honorable James Harlan, Secretary of the Interior, the James Watts of his generation. In the text, however, Twain ignored the usual cognomen clues (Figs. 15 & 16). Twain's calculating Mr. Noble, on the other hand, bears little resemblance in either visage or surname to the Honorable

CHAIRMAN OF THE COMMITTEE.

Fig. 13. CHAIRMAN OF THE COMMITTEE.

Fig. 14. RALPH BUCKLAND.

BRO. BALAAM.

Fig. 15. BRO. BALAAM.

HON. JAMES HARLAN, SECRETARY OF THE INTERIOR.—[Photographed by Brady.]

HON. JAMES HARLAN, SECRETARY OF THE INTERIOR.
Fig. 16.

MR. NOBLE ASKS QUESTIONS.

Fig. 17. MR. NOBLE ASKS QUESTIONS.

SCENE IN THE KANSAS STATE-HOUSE WHEN THE BRIBE MONEY WAS HANDED TO THE PRESIDING OFFICER.
[FROM A SKETCH BY H. WORRALL.]

SCENE IN THE KANSAS STATE-HOUSE WHEN THE BRIBE MONEY WAS HANDED TO THE PRESIDING OFFICER.
Fig. 18.

HON A. M. YORK, MR. POMEROY'S ACCUSER.
[FROM A PHOTOGRAPH BY J. LEE KNIGHT, TOPEKA, KANSAS.]

Fig. 19.   HON. A. M. YORK, MR. POMEROY'S ACCUSER.

HON. OAKES AMES.—FROM A PHOTOGRAPH BY GARDNER, WASHINGTON, D. C.—[SEE PAGE 130.]

Fig. 20. HON. OAKES AMES.

MR. TROLLOP THINKS IT OVER

Fig. 21. MR. TROLLOP THINKS IT OVER.

AT HEADQUARTERS.

Fig. 22. AT HEADQUARTERS.

A. M. York, Pomeroy's arch enemy in the Kansas City State House bribe scenario. And Twain's narrative in the text is also a mixed bag of the facts and fancies surrounding the famous scandal (Figs. 17, 18, & 19).[18]

Visual and verbal connections become more confusing with other characters such as the corrupt congressman, Mr. Fairoaks, whose antics can be traced to the like shenanigans of Oakes Ames of Credit-Mobilier fame. There is no engraving of Mr. Fairoaks in the first edition, but the last syllable of his name was one of the clues that enabled Mark Twain's contemporaries to identify him as Oakes Ames. Real confusion sets in, however, with a

Fig. 23. WILLIAM BIGLER.

JOLLY GOOD COMPANY.

Fig. 24. JOLLY GOOD COMPANY.

possible textual parallel between the real Oakes Ames and
Twain's Mr. Trollop, whose facial characteristics are not those of
the famous Mr. Ames, with or without hair (Figs. 20 & 21).[19]

In other areas there is no confusion, for Mark Twain included actual people in the fiction without bothering to change
names or even exaggerate the circumstances. Senator William
Bigler's features closely match the appearance of his namesake,
Pennsylvania's Senator Bigler. In addition, both Twain's fictional character and the real Bigler had been linked to the notoriously corrupt railroad squabbles in the Pennsylvania state legislature.
It took little detective work to connect the two (Figs. 22 & 23).
Also, President Grant is more than recognizable in a small cut
shared with Colonel Sellers (Fig. 24).[20]

Unfortunately, lost are many contemporary figures whose
identities are obvious from the narrative but whose features are
not displayed in visual form in the book; for example, George S.
Boutwell, mentioned by Mark Twain as "having good fiscal
policy but lacking courage." And the pages cite the complete
Tweed Ring: Wm. M. Weed, the New York City politician who
stole $20,000 from the city ("Boss" William Marcy Tweed), the
"controller" (Richard "Slippery Dick" Connolly), the "board of
audit" (Peter "Brains" Sweeney), and the "mayor" (Mayor A.
"Elegant Oakey" Hall).[21] It seems incredible that no one suggested the gifted Henry Stephens copy from his many sketches
of some of these same people in *(Burlesque) Autobiography*.
The editors and the illustrators, through careless craftsmanship,
ignorance, and/or insufficient supervision, left unfulfilled the
basic concept for the book. They failed to play on all the images
paralleling the people in the narrative which made it a true *Tale
of To-day*.

Bliss also missed the chance to use caricature in his promotional campaign. Instead of informing the press and writing ads
including illustrations that would patently reveal the exposé of
prominent persons in the book, Bliss's publicity buried in small
print hints that *The Gilded Age* was written to satirize the times.
Bliss's press releases generalized that the humorous narrative was
leveled at public topics, persons, and follies of the day.[22] There
were no fireworks, just a small flash when he did prominently
feature one of Hoppin's full-page prints, LAURA RECEIVES
DILLWORTHY'S [sic] BLESSING, as the frontispiece for the
prospectus. The readers of the prospectus were left to make
their own discoveries of caricature after they subscribed for and

received their own book.

To their credit, the reviewers, if not the general public, reveled in the match-up game. Most critics immediately recognized Pomeroy and Nye—and seemed pleased to say so. "Pomeroy," said the reviewer for the Boston *Saturday Evening Gazette*, "figures as Senator Dilworthy in the volume;"[23] "Nobody will fail to see Senator Pomeroy through this hypothetical Dilworthy,"[24] wrote the reviewer for Pomeroy's (no relation) *Democrat*. The New York *World* reviewer sang much the same refrain: "Senator Dilworthy, for example, will be as readily recognized as though the true name had been used by Messrs. Clemens and Warner."[25]   From the New York *Evening Mail*: "His facility in prayer-meetings is faithfully set before the reader, and his last experience with the Kansas legislature is literally narrated."[26]   And again from the *Mail*, "Nye is shown in his franking operation with exceeding humor. . . . Some of the picutres are very well done."[27]

It is odd that action and illustration were not more tightly linked throughout the book, especially when such meticulous planning and the hiring of talented caricaturists had been worked out in the initial stages before publication. Clemens, away in England during the printing and proofreading, may have followed his usual pattern and left most of the finishing details to others— to Warner and Bliss in this case. While *The Gilded Age* was proceeding through the manufacturing process, Clemens had indeed hurried to England to lecture and supervise the English publication of the book. The pirating of his books in foreign markets and the problems with design—both of his previous works had been issued abroad without illustration—had become matters of great concern to the author.

Bliss, busy with one of his heaviest issuing seasons in years, probably neglected to instruct the artists on sketching real parallels to match the people in the fiction. Or, he may consciously have chosen to avoid a confrontation with prominent political figures. Whatever the reasons, caricature did not work well as the illustrating device for *The Gilded Age.*

Even while overseas, however, Mark Twain had maintained a limited control over the portrayal of at least one character. In letters to both Warner and Bliss, he was most explicit in his instructions concerning the physical appearance of Colonel Sellers. Twain's model for the Colonel was, of course, James Lampton, his mother's favorite cousin. A detailed description of this lovable, laughable, old soul probably came from the author's sister, Pamela Moffett. In a letter written in the early 1870's Clemens had written to Pamela urging her to quiz cousin Mollie about the entire family:

> I wish you would get all the gossip you can out of Mollie about Cousin James Lampton & Family, *without her knowing it is I that want it.* I want every little trifling detail, about how they look & dress, & what they say, & how the house is furnished—& the various ages & characters of the tribe.[28]

Pamela Moffett's reply to her brother's letter has not survived; but she was always a faithful correspondent, and she may well have been the one who coined the now well-known clichés by dutifully sending Clemens descriptions he could use in delineating Sellers' eccentrities in speech (the famous "There's a million in it"), the household furnishings (the remarkable clock whose time was always twenty-two minutes past anything), and the family diet (turnips, bread, and butter), though Twain undoubtedly elaborated on the details. She also probably commented on Lampton's attire.

Be that as it may, Clemens' sent instructions about the illustrations to Warner, Warner then relayed them to Bliss, and Bliss in turn passed them on to the artists. Though this was a long and precarious chain of communication, it shows Mark Twain was attempting to get the accurate visual nuances for the Colonel. One Clemens letter contains these instructions:

> For goodness sake let no artist make of Sellers anything but a *gentleman.* . . . Even his dress (vide the scene where Washington first visits him at Hawkeye) is carefully kept & has the expression about it of being the latest charm in excellency of that kind. He always wears a stovepipe hat. . . . He must not be *distorted or caricatured* in any way in order to make a "funny" picture. Make him plain & simple. (The original was tall & slender.) However, I believe we have hinted that Sellers is portly, in one place—which is just as well.[29]

Clemens truly loved the pathetic old man, and his instructions showed that he wanted the illustrators to resist any temptation to make the character appear ridiculous. True Williams' sketch of the scene in which Washington arrives in Hawkeye demonstrates the special care taken by the illustrators to follow Clemens' instructions—to portray the Colonel accurately and to preserve his elegant style. Here Williams gives us the engaging Sellers smile and ever-present stove-pipe hat, adding (and the addition is supported by the text) the false fumbling for the non-existent tip. And this sketch is not atypical: throughout the novel the illustrators, as directed, treated Sellers with respect (Fig. 25).

Another of Mark Twain's major concerns was his unique layout of the Salt Lick Branch of the Pacific Railroad. In the manuscript the author had combined the Colonel's descriptive speech about the line with a rough sketch of the route for the imaginary road; from Glouchburg (later changed to Slouchburg, represented by a lumpy potato) to Bloody Run (pictured as an inkpot and quill). Twain's manuscript contained both the informative text and an interlinear map he had drawn. The map was a delightfully amateur pen-and-ink doodle in Twain's inimitable style (Fig. 26).

Examining the first draft of the railroad layout, both authors agreed that a more detailed drawing should be worked up.

COL. SELLERS ENLIGHTENING THE BOHEMIANS.

Fig. 25. COL. SELLERS ENLIGHTENING THE BOHEMIANS.

Fig. 26. CLEMENS' INTERLINEAR "MAP."

Mark Twain resketched his ideas in one continuous illustration on a special long sheet of paper.[30] He had pasted a number of sheets of paper together, drawn his fanciful rail line, numbered it 622, and folded and inserted it in the manuscript after page 624, indicating by this placement where he wanted the final print to appear. The text on the preceding page read: "Now here you are with your railroad complete, and showing its continuation to Hallelujah, and thence to Corruptionville."[31] On the bottom of the page Twain had written: "(Insert Map)."[32] Apparently, the second long layout of the rail line has not survived. The final printed version for the book, unsigned by the artist, shows that the illustrator faithfully followed Twain's rough draft detail for detail; from the waiter (an early term for a small serving tray) that was to represent St. Louis, to the rat trap (with comic connotations) meant for Napoleon (Fig. 27).

Because the final print of the map was an over-size drawing it had to be carefully folded and tipped in by hand so that it would fit and face page 246 where Mark Twain has Sellers describe the route. Though this last-minute bindery process was extremely expensive, hand-tipping pages into an initial press run of 50,000 books, Bliss complied with Twain's wishes. Since the production costs were growing daily—Bliss would claim that he spent nearly $10,000 on the plates of the book[33]—the editor prudently turned the whimsical map into a promotional ploy. In the circular he told prospective buyers: "Go wild over the haps and mishaps of the fine corps of engineers engaged in the laying out of the 'Salt Lick Branch of the Pacific R. R.' as it appears on the characteristic map of it which the book contains."[34]

The costly folded carte struck a responsive chord with at least one of the novel's reviewers:

> Who else [but Mark Twain] would have so contrived to mix up civil engineering and a schedule of the table and toilet furniture of a Western speculator, A. D. 1873? In a thousand years, this cut will have immense antiquarian value, like the paintings of utensils at Pompeii.[35]

Perhaps the map will never rival the art or artifacts of Pompeii; however, in a curious way the reviewer was prophetic. The map did become a sought-after collector's item, although not in the critic's cynical sense. Since the tipped-in map appeared in only the first printing of the first edition, bibliographers

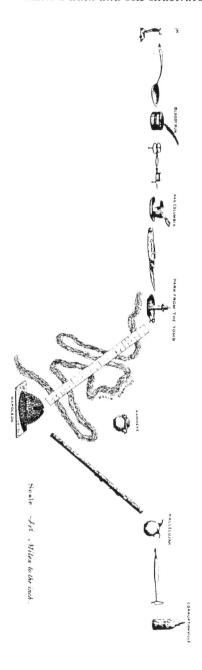

MAP OF THE SALT LICK BRANCH OF THE PACIFIC R. R.
Fig. 27.

would subsequently validate a first state-first edition by the presence of this folded page or by evidence of the page having been at one time tipped in. Readers who had to make do with later printings of the first edition would be denied visual aids when trying to picture the peculiar combination of kitchen utensils and other household objects that represented Sellers' ill-fated rail line.

Another puzzling item that crops up in some copies of the first-state editions of *The Gilded Age* is a tipped-in "fake" title page. According to Merle Johnson, a few copies have surfaced with a title page dated 1873 (*The Gilded Age* copy was filed in Washington 6 January 1874) *without* the name of one of the illustrators, the elusive George G. White who was responsible for the CITY OF BABYLON tail piece discussed earlier. Various explanations have been offered for the 1873 dating: subscription agents arranging *sub rosa* sales of their copies of the book to bookstores, an 1873 date mark inserted into a few early copies meant only for reviewers, or perhaps a technique Bliss may have devised to make it possible for a few books to invade the trade market.[36] The omission of White's name in only these random few and never again in subsequent printings of the book has been noted by bibliographers but never explained.

An additional example of how frustrating or helpful illustration can be for bibliographers involves a "missing" print. On page 403 of the first state there is a half page of text, with the remaining sheet blank. The "List of Illustrations" cites, even in this state, PHILIP LEAVING LAURA. TAIL PIECE (Fig. 28). The appropriate cut was supplied only for the second-state printing of the book. The missing print became another authentic hallmark signaling the first state—similar to the second Napoleon in the second printing of *The Innocents Abroad*.[37]

Another tail piece featuring Laura, occurring in all states of the book (though of little interest to historical scholarship), has delightfully naughty overtones. In this section of the narrative Mark Twain is describing Laura Hawkins' life style in Washington society, emphasizing her conversational ability and her literary tastes. This tail piece suggests that Laura may have been practicing a more tantalizing occupation (Fig. 29). The full-breasted statue's expression was undoubtedly ignored by both editors and authors in proofreading sessions.

The Gilded Age was copyrighted and announced in the press as early as April 1873—which may explain why some copies

Fig. 28. TAIL PIECE.

Fig. 29. TAIL PIECE.

From Official Report of Trial

Laura D. Fair

Fig. 30. LAURA D. FAIR.

had an 1873 title-page dating. Clemens had been confident that the book would be pushed through production and issued by fall. In the pattern of his previous publications, of course, the American edition was published later than expected, partly because of an argument about English copyright which resulted in an official publication date only a few days before Christmas.[38]

In England, worried about copyright, Clemens had been trying to ensure simultaneous publication for an illustrated English and American edition. All through late summer his letters prodded Bliss about pictures and casts:

> We shall issue a copyright edition of the novel here in fine style . . .; send sheets and duplicate casts of the pictures by successive steamers always. And send these casts and proofs along as fast as you get a signature done. . . . State as nearly as you can the exact day at which you can publish.[39]

Clemens' pleading had its reward. For the first time an illustrated Mark Twain book had a "simultaneous publication in the United States and England . . . and the issuance in the two countries occurred according to plan, apparently within forty-eight hours."[40] Routledge, Clemens' English publisher, printed five hundred of a fully illustrated, three-volume edition on 23 December 1873; eight thousand of a cheaper edition were issued in 1874.[41]

The novel, with its specific parallels to American society and politics, had little appeal for a British audience. For the English critics the book as a *roman à clef* was confusing. They were irritated by the authors' introduction of too many characters, people known to and therefore able to pique the interest of the state-side reader but remaining largely anonymous to overseas readers. The reviewer for the *Athenaeum* complained that the illustrations were poor and inaccurate, and that they did not greatly assist the English reader to identify the too numerous characters in the novel. He had serious objections, too, to having so much of the dirty linen of "American speculation [displayed] for the benefit of foreign readers."[42] The English were used to and appreciative of Mark Twain's witty prose. They also expected the same quality and wit in the illustrations. Unfortunately, *The Gilded Age* had only a diluted

Mark Twain humor combined with the mediocre illustrating talent of the American artist. Inevitably, the reviews in the English press were, on the whole, negative.

Surprisingly, reviews by American critics were also mixed. Though the critics' love affair with Mark Twain was diminishing they were willing and able to appreciate the concept. Unlike their overseas colleagues, the local reviewers made the fiction-to-real-life connections. "Seventeen out of thirty-eight reviews, or nearly half, acknowledged that actual persons and events were portrayed, and nine of these seventeen named names."[43]

Along with the Dilworthy-Nye identifications mentioned earlier, the critics spotted Brother Balaam as Senator Harlan, pointing out that his link with Indian operations was significantly suggested.[44] They also accurately pegged John Graham as counterpart to Twain's Mr. Braham, the "most successful criminal lawyer, [who] is as palpable to the reader of 'The Gilded Age' as he is to the frequenters of our criminal courts."[45] A most perceptive critic noted that the characters were not mere caricatures, but realities, and that the more prominent ones were easily recognized. " 'Weed' is BOSS TWEED, and 'Senator Dilworthy' is . . . 'Old Subsidy Pom.,' . . . Poor Laura Hawkins, who fascinates everyone who sees her, is another LAURA FAIR of San Francisco fame" (Fig. 30).[46]

In these early reviews and through the history of the novel the book has been roundly condemned for its lack of cohesiveness. Nevertheless, at the time of publication, the novelty of the paired authors as well as some curiosity about the political satire outweighed the weakness of construction. The edition was an immediate best seller.[47] The original intention of Clemens and Warner was to write a book that would sell, and this they had done. The reviewers understood the motivation, recognized that the book would appeal to a general readership, and larded their critical comments with phrases like "a strong savor of lucre," and "It will sell like 'hot cakes.' "[48]

While the book was still selling extremely well, Clemens wrote his fellow author, Thomas Bailey Aldrich, ruminating about a seeming paradox—that subscription books, despite their consistently low quality, brought in unbelievably high rewards to their authors:

> There is one discomfort which I fear a man must put up
> with when he publishes by subscription, and that is

wretched paper and vile engravings. I fancy the publisher don't make a very large pile when he pays his
author 10 p. c. You notice that the Gilded Age is rather
a rubbishy looking book; well, the sale has now reached
about 50,000 copies—so the royalty now due the authorship is about $18,000.[49]

Clemens wasn't the only complainant, and an increasingly touchy
Bliss tried valiantly to counter the charges about sub-standard
quality in an advertisement written just before the issuing of
The Gilded Age:

> The most expensive books issued are those which have
> the engravings worked in with the text. The reasons
> are these:—To make the cuts effective, it requires a
> great many and a large outlay. We have expended on
> the plates for this book [*The Gilded Age*] nearly
> $10,000. . . . We claim that we sell you books with
> from two hundred to three hundred engravings, finely
> printed on extra fine paper, and most firmly bound, as
> low as you can buy any book equal in *weight, size,* and
> *popularity,* containing but few if any cuts, at any book-
> store; while you will be asked there for books illustrated
> as are our $3.50 ones (if they have any such) at least
> $5 or $6.[50]

Despite this plea (with its interesting emphasis on weight and
size), Clemens felt that Bliss had not lived up to the assurance
of quality spelled out in the contract.

Mark Twain's dream of an exquisitely designed book was a
shambles. Without Nast's talent—and Nast's name on the spine
would have helped later sales—the original scheme misfired.
Had it been possible to commission Hoppin for all the sketches,
the book might have been more attractive. Certainly his unmistakable resemblances and his careful attention to detail set
his work above much of that done by other artists. Yet even
Hoppin's prints suffered from the rough, poor-quality paper and,
sometimes, the inconsistency of the engravers, who worked with
painstaking care on only selected cuts. Stephens was a clever
cartoonist, but his talents were not put to full use—partly,
one suspects, because of the usual slipshod supervision in Bliss's
production-line process. Williams, to his credit, contributed his

workman-like best, even though he undoubtedly felt that his part in illustrating the book was far smaller than his talents warranted. All in all, the end result of using numerous illustrators was artistic mush: inconsistent characterization (Laura looking alternately like the belle of the ball and a middle-aged matron), and shifting styles (from finely delineated lines to heavily penned cardboard cutouts).

Indeed, Clemens made money out of both the English and American editions, but his desire for profit was fast becoming secondary in his list of priorities. In the last paragraph of his letter to Aldrich he suggests a new role for himself:

> Now I think seriously of *printing* my own next book and publishing it thro' this same subscription house. It will thus be a mighty starchy book, but I reckon I won't get so much money out of it.[51]

Clemens' forecast would be only too correct, and he would enter a period of "financial frenzy" as he tried to take over control of production for his next novel, *The Adventures of Tom Sawyer*.

Notes

[1] SLC to EB, 3 May 1873, *MT&EB*, p. 75. Also in *MTLP*, pp. 75-76. These plans for talking about the publication of *The Gilded Age* may have included George Routledge of George Routledge and Sons, the firm slated to issue the English edition. Mr. Routledge was in Hartford on that date.

[2] *The Gilded Age* contract, 8 May 1873, MTP. A sentence later the contract specified, "The engravings inserted to be mutually acceptable to said Warner & to E. Bliss Jur. Prest. of said American Publishing Co." Samuel Clemens was not listed as part of the supervising staff according to the contract, perhaps because he planned to spend time, after manuscript was complete, in England.

[3] SLC to EB, 4 March 1873, *MTLP*, p. 75.

[4] "Twain's account [of Pomeroy's career] in *The Gilded Age*, far from being overdrawn, is a surprisingly exact copy. This can easily be

shown by a comparison of Dilworthy's character with that of Pomeroy, and of the details of the exposure and investigation in the novel and in newspapers and government records of the time" (Albert R. Kitzhaber, "Mark Twain's Use of the Pomeroy Case in *The Gilded Age,*" *Modern Language Quarterly,* XV [March 1954], 42-56). "The Laura Fair trial had been headlined intermittently from June 1871 until January 1873. . . . Her prolonged series of court trials and appeals was emblazoned in American headlines from coast to coast" (Bryant Morey French, "Mark Twain, Laura D. Fair and the New York Criminal Courts," *American Quarterly,* XVI [Winter 1964], 545-561). Further connections are made in Arthur L. Vogelbank, "Mark Twain and the Tammany Ring," *PMLA,* LXX (March 1955), 71.

[5] SLC to EB, 4 March 1873, *CL 3.* Published in *MTLP,* p. 75.

[6] Isabel Lyon file 1937, Vassar. Ideas about a possible lecture also in *MTB,* 321.

[7] Thomas Nast to SLC, 24 April 1871, Berg Collection. In reply, Clemens sent Nast a number of pieces, offering generous leeway: "Take any sketch you please and you are the man to make the selection, because you can tell what will illustrate best" (SLC to Thomas Nast [after 24 April 1871], *CL 3*). This correspondence resulted in the collaboration of Clemens and the caricaturist in Nast's Almanac, 1872 and 1873. Clemens responded to Nast on finally receiving a copy: "The Almanac has come and I have enjoyed those pictures with all my soul and body" (SLC to Thomas Nast, 17 December 1872, *CL 3*).

[8] *MTLP,* p. 75, note 2. Also in Albert Bigelow Paine, *Thomas Nast: His Period and His Pictures* (New York: 1904), p. 263. Nast replied to Clemens concerning the English book 15 December 1872. The book on England was never written, as Clemens was too "social" in London and unwilling to offend his British friends (see *MTB,* 465). Ten years later Clemens wrote again proposing a joint lecture tour: "Therefore I now propose to you what you proposed to me in November, 1867—ten years ago . . . That you should stand on the platform and make pictures, and I stand by you and blackguard the audience" (SLC to Thomas Nast, 12 November 1877, Isabel Lyon file 1937, Vassar, TS in MTP).

[9] *MT&EB,* p. 77. "A receipt for $150 for an illustration, 'A Spray of Box,' from William S. [sic] Smedley is in Yale" (*MT&EB,* p. 196, note 16). The substituted PLAYING TO WIN in on page 337 of the first edition and is not a good characterization of either Laura or Mr. Buckstone. In other cuts Buckstone does resemble his real-life counterpart, Ralph Buckland. Interestingly, W. T. Smedley later drew six full-page illustrations for a two-volume edition of *The Gilded Age* for Harper and Brothers.

[10] Hamilton, I: 152.

[11] "We prize this copy most on account of the autograph" [William

Dean Howells, *Their Wedding Journey,* Boston: James Osgood and Company, 1872) (*MTHL,* 1:10). Illustrations were by Hoppin. Olivia's choice is cited by Alan Gribben: "Hoppin, Augustus (1828-1896). *Ups and Downs on Land and Water.* Boston: James R. Osgood & Co., 1871. On 22 December 1873 Olivia Clemens was billed by Brown & Gross, Hartford booksellers, for '1 Ups & Downs $10.00' " (Alan Gribben, *Mark Twain's Library: A Reconstruction,* I [Boston: G. K. Hall and Co., 1980], 323). The book was also serialized in the *Atlantic* with illustrations by Hoppin.

[12] Hamilton, I: 224. Hoppin produced 16 full-page prints.

[13] "The title-page states that Stephens is one of the illustrators, but none of the illustrations appear to bear his signature" (Hamilton, I: 208-210; II: 135-137). "The caricatures of H. L. Stephens in *Vanity Fair* entitle him to be ranked at or very near the top of the list of cartoonists who were prominent before Nast. . . . He had good ideas, and he drew smoothly; but he lacked the vigorous feeling of Nast" (Frank Luther Mott, *A History of American Magazines 1850-1865,* II [Cambridge: Harvard University Press, 1938], 523).

[14] *"The title-page occurs in two major forms:* 1: The genuine title-page which carries the statement, *Fully Illustrated From New Designs By Hoppin, Stephens, Williams, White, Etc., Etc,* . . . which carries the statement, *Fully Illustrated From New Designs By Hoppin, Stephens, Williams, Etc., Etc.* Note absence of the name *White.* The title-page is printed from types quite unlike that used for the genuine title-page. . . . In the case of so popular an author as Mark Twain retail booksellers were most anxious to secure copies of his books for sale across the counter and agents or canvassers often arranged the *sub rosa* sale of books to retail shops. . . . Study of both states of the title-page . . . leads to the inescapable conclusion that the 'forged' title-page was produced by The American Publishing Company. . . . The publishers may have violated their own injunction regarding sales to bookshops" (*BAL* II: 184). On the other hand, Merle Johnson states: "It is almost certain that this [variant title-page] was printed by a firm desiring to evade subscription regulations governing the sale of the book and substituted for the original page. . . . It lacks the name of one of the illustrators, White, and . . . further, the type is different from that of other printings. Mr. Bliss of the American Publishing Company certified that no such fonts of type were in the possession of his company. Added certainty is given the restriction-evasion theory by the fact that numerous other copies exist with a rectangular slit at the bottom of the page where a firm name had been cut out" (*BMT,* p. 18). The "White" tail piece appears on page 167 of the first edition and also on page 60 of *Beyond the Mississippi.*

[15] "Elisha Bliss's illustrators worked directly from pictures of the

bearded and fatherly-looking Senator" (Mark Twain and Charles Dudley Warner, *The Gilded Age: A Tale of To-day,* intro. Justin Kaplan, New York, Trident Press, 1964, p. xv). Hereafter cited as *The Gilded Age, 1964.* Hoppin's full-page Dilworthy prints appear facing pages 480 and 389 of the first edition. Hamlin Hill mentioned the Dilworthy-Pomeroy name connections in *MT&EB,* p. 75.

[16] Mark Twain and Charles Dudley Warner, *The Gilded Age: A Tale of To-day* (Hartford: The American Publishing Company, 1874), p. 326. Hereafter cited as *The Gilded Age, 1874.* Nye's features appear in cuts on pages 324 & 326 of the first edition. "Nye is shown in his franking operation with exceeding humor" (New York *Evening Mail,* "Notices of the Press," Documents 1873, MTP). "Abuse of the franking privilege is alluded to no less than three times during the novel. The custom was prevalent and the subject of public comment" (*The Gilded Age: A Tale of To-day,* ed. Bryant Morey French (Indianapolis: Bobbs Merrill Company, Inc., 1972], intro. xxvii). Hereafter cited as *The Gilded Age, 1972.* See also Robert L. Gale, *Plots and Characters In the Works of Mark Twain,* II (Hamden, Connecticut: Anchor Books, 1973), 1090. Hereafter cited as Gale, *Characters.*

[17] "Twain's published letters and newspaper correspondences are replete with deriding references to Nye" (Bryant Morey French, *Mark Twain and The Gilded Age: The Book That Named An Era* [Dallas: Southern Methodist University, 1965], p. 92). Hereafter cited as *MT&TGA.*

[18] *MT&TGA,* p. 139. French documents most of the identifiable politicians.

[19] French writes about Mr. Trollop: "Mr. Trollop, on the other hand, appears to be nothing more than a convenient foil for Laura and a catchall for parodies on congressional bills" (*MT&TGA,* p. 136). But in a note French admits, "It should be added, however, that Twain's description of Trollop's appearance as a 'grave, carefully dressed and very respectable-looking man, with a bald head, standing collar, and old-fashioned watch seals' indicates that he may have had a real person in mind" (*MT&TGA,* p. 310, note 79).

[20] President Grant's features appear in a cut on page 356, JOLLY GOOD COMPANY. The cut of the fictional Bigler appears on page 251. French makes the connection that Bigler was a member of "the 'great firm of Pennybacker, Bigler & Small, railroad contractors,' who in planning the financing of the Tunkhannock, Rattlesnake, and Youngwomanstown Railroad proposes to 'arrange things' in the Pennsylvania legislature. . . . Here is an obvious allusion to Governor, and sometime Senator, William Bigler of Pennsylvania, who had been involved earlier in the contest between the Pennsylvania Railroad and the Baltimore and Ohio to

secure the state charter authorizing incorporation" (*MT&TGA*, p. 139). Also see Gale, *Characters* II: 721.

[21] In his introduction to the Bobbs Merrill edition of *The Gilded Age,* French notes: "The Tweed Ring figures in the novel, indeed, in barely disguised form. . . . There are the "controler," "board of audit," and "Mayor," who unquestionably refer to the Ring's quadrumverate in control of the New York City government: Mayor A. 'Elegant Oakey' Hall, Controller Richard 'Slippery Dick' Connolly, Treasurer Peter B. 'Brains' Sweeney, and William Marcy 'Boss' Tweed himself" (*The Gilded Age* [1972], p. xxxiv). French also identifies John Braham as John Graham, p. xxvii; Judge O'Shaunnessy as Judge John McCunn, p. xxviii; Mr. Fairoaks as Oakes Ames, p. xxxi; Senator Noble as Senator York, p. xxxi; Senator Harlan as "Brother Balaam," p. xxxii; and Patrick O'Riley as Thomas Murphy, p. xxxiv. French also cites the fact that in the Warner manuscript a character named "Schaick at first is called 'Gold,' a circumstance that suggests that Warner originally had in mind Jay Gould. . . . The description, however, which has not been altered, does not touch on Gould's most salient characteristics, and 'Gold' may be no more than a symbolic cognomen for a person of great wealth" (*MT&GA*, p. 310, note 88).

[22] Prospectus, *The Gilded Age*, Documents 1874, MTP. On the final pages of this prospectus are these words: "It [*The Gilded Age*] was written expressly to *fit* the *times*, its satire and humor being leveled at the public topics, persons, and follies of the day." The remaining promotional material focused on the "joint production of the two famous authors." Justin Kaplan states: "With a wisdom not supported by the results, Bliss's promotion for the book scarcely mentioned its topical content, not to say its drift, and emphasized the novelty of two prominent authors working together. As a vendor of entertaining and edifying books he was bound to fear his authors had carried their satire too far, and many of the reviewers shared this feeling" (*The Gilded Age*, 1964, p. xxi).

[23] Boston *Saturday Evening Gazette*, "Notices of the Press," Documents 1873, MTP.

[24] Pomeroy's *Democrat*, "Notices of the Press," Documents 1873, MTP.

[25] New York *World*, "Notices of the Press," Documents 1873, MTP.

[26] New York *Evening Mail*, "Notices of the Press," Documents 1873, MTP.

[27] New York *Evening Mail*, "Notices of the Press," Documents 1873, MTP.

[28] *Mark Twain, Business Man*, ed. Samuel Charles Webster (Boston: Little Brown and Company, 1946), p. 120.

[29]Samuel Clemens' autograph letter in Rare Books and Special Collections, Hamilton Collection, Princeton University Library. "In the Princeton copy of *The Gilded Age* are 'pp. 3 to 6 inclusive of an autograph letter signed Samuel L. Clemens in which he describes Sellers. . .and gives instructions as to how the artist [A. Hoppin] should depict him' " (Hamilton, I: 155). It is doubtful that Hoppin was the artist here.

[30]*MT&TGA*, "Appendix E," pp. 269-270.

[31]*The Gilded Age*, 1874, p. 246.

[32]*MT&TGA*, p. 342, note 3. The folded map appeared facing page 246 in the first edition-first state.

[33]In 1873 Bliss published a Circular defending the subscription book and its costs. In it he stated: "To make the cuts effective, it requires a great many and a large outlay. We have expended on the plates for this book [*The Gilded Age*] nearly $10,000" ("Circular," Documents 1873, MTP).

[34]"Circular," *The Gilded Age*, Documents 1873, MTP.

[35]*MT&TGA*, p. 269. Originally printed in *Old and New*, IX (March 1874), 386-388.

[36]*BAL*, II: 184. See note 14 above.

[37]"P. 403: In the earliest printing there is no illustration. In later printings an illustration is present" (*BAL*, II: 185). "The real test of the first edition of *The Gilded Age* may be found at p. 403 which in the first state does not carry a picture of *Philip Leaving Flora* [sic]. This illustration, however, is called for in the list of illustrations. This cut was later supplied" (*BMT*, p. 18). Johnson mistakes Flora for Laura in this citation. It is also interesting to note that Blanck finds in *The Gilded Age*, first edition-first state, "P. xvi: the final illustration is number 211. Later 212" (*BAL*, II: 185). These illustrations in the first edition are: 211, THE SICK CHAMBER (full page print) *Face Page*, 570, executed by Hoppin; illustration 212, ALICE (inserted cut), 573, executed by True Williams.

[38]"Apparently exasperated at seeing the market slip away, Bliss ignored Twain's instructions about copyright and called for the binding of *The Gilded Age* to begin in time to capitalize on the Christmas season. On December 11 the first 480 cloth copies arrived, and by the end of the year 12,446 copies were bound and being delivered to customers" (*MT&EB*, p. 78).

[39]SLC to EB, 16 July [1873], *MTLP*, p. 77.

[40]*MT&TGA*, p. 264.

[41]*MTinEng*, p. 43.

[42]*MTinEng*, p. 44.

[43]*MT&TGA*, p. 86.

[44]New York *Mail*, "Notices of the Press," Documents 1873, MTP.

[45]New York *World*, "Notices of the Press," Documents 1873, MTP.

[46]Unidentifiable original newspaper notice, "Notices of the Press," Documents 1873, MTP. Other reviews in the Document file in MTP: Philadelphia *Sunday Press* and the Rochester New York *Union Advertiser.* Welland cites English reviews in *The Standard,* 29 December 1873 and *The Athenaeum,* 10 January 1874 (*MTinEng,* p. 252, note 14).

[47]"After the 12,446 copies which had been bound between December 11 and the end of 1873 came from the bindery, the sales remained brisk for two more months: in January the total rose to 26,821; in February, to 35,745. These sales were worth celebrating. Neither of the earlier American Publishing Company books had sold so well in the first two and a half months. But in March, 1874, sales dropped to only 1,000 copies, and at the end of its first full year *The Gilded Age* had sold only 50,325 copies, 15,000 less than *Roughing It* and almost 20,000 less than *Innocents* in their first years" (*MT&EB,* pp. 84-85).

[48]"Notices of the Press," Documents 1873, MTP.

[49]*MTLP,* p. 81.

[50]*MT&EB,* p. 9.

[51]*MTLP,* p. 81.

List of Illustrations: *The Gilded Age*

Chapter V

Sketches, New & Old and *Tom Sawyer*

"The illustrations seem to lack the humor that
pervades the text."

In 1874 and 1875 Mark Twain worked hard on two subscription books—*Sketches, New & Old* (1875) and *The
Adventures of Tom Sawyer* (finished in mid-1875 but not published until 1876). Both of these books, like the other subscription books he had published with Bliss, were fully illustrated.
   Undoubtedly, Mark Twain saw the book of sketches as a
kind of pot-boiler. Since *The Gilded Age* was not selling well, he
was anxious to have something on the market. Getting together
a book of sketches—most of them previously published—promised to be easier than getting out another novel or another
book of travel. His plan was to recycle some of his old sketches,
add illustrations to give the book size, and publish it as a "trade"
book rather than one marked "sold only by subscription."
   There were to be sixty-three sketches in the book that Mark
Twain had ready for 1875 publication, but only seven of them
were new. It was not Elisha Bliss's policy to issue a subscription
book that included so much old material, but he was willing to
bend a policy in order to avoid losing a writer of Twain's potential. Thus, when Twain informed Bliss that he was considering
publishing sketches as a trade book, Bliss pulled an old 1871 contract out of his files and strongly suggested that if Twain was
going to publish any work, he was still legally bound to this
almost forgotten agreement. That settled the matter of where to
publish.
   Bliss agreed to accept the sketch book in fulfillment of the
1871 contract. He also agreed that the book should be illustrated—almost routinely he handed Mark Twain's printer's copy
over to True Williams. There was no discussion about alternate
illustrators. Bliss, for his part, gave little or no instruction to
Williams. The artist did, however, receive a number of suggestions from Mark Twain on at least four of the stories: "The

Petrified Man," "Some Learned Fables for Good Old Boys and Girls," "The 'Blind Letter' Department, London P. O.," and the Jumping Frog story.

"The Petrified Man" had already appeared in several unillustrated versions. It had been printed originally in the *Territorial Enterprise* on 4 October 1862, and was reprinted in as many as twelve California and Nevada papers. Mark Twain recalled with amusement that most of the papers seemed to copy his admitted "hoax" in good faith.[1] This time, in order to clarify the pivotal point of the tale for his readers, Twain prepared printer's copy for the book and wrote in the margin: "Make a picture of him [the petrified man] " (Fig. 1).[2]

Fig. 1. THE PETRIFIED MAN.

The clue to an appreciation of Mark Twain's joke in the story lay, of course, in his description of the position of the hands of the petrified man:

> the right thumb resting against the side of the nose; the left thumb partially supported the chin, the forefinger pressing the inner corner of the left eye and drawing it partly open; the right eye was closed, and the fingers of the right hand spread apart.[3]

When Mark Twain retold this story in a much revised form in his new book of sketches, he described the indecent gesture in such a way that not even the most casual reader was likely to miss his point: "his right tumb was against the side of his nose . . . [and] the left thumb was hooked into the right little finger; the fingers of the left hand were spread like those of the right."[4] When Williams "made a picture of him," in accordance with Twain's marginal note (Fig. 1), he followed the unambiguous revised version, not the intentionally misleading original.

Another suggestion by Mark Twain instructed the artist on relevant ideas for illustrating "Some Learned Fables." Twain even went so far as to sketch doodles in his text. For the first part of the story the author's marginalia indicated that he wanted a picture of the procession of his animal expedition and he marked the space for the desired cut.[5] Williams obliged with a whimsical parade of insects, worms, reptiles, and other creatures (Figs. 2 & 3). For the second part of the fable Twain drew a set of signs. Williams followed the author's detailed design but polished up the art work (Figs. 4 & 5).

For "The 'Blind Letter' Department, London P. O." Mark Twain requested that Williams included among his illustrations facsimile drawings of some of the "envelopes that pass through the [London post-office] with queer pictures drawn upon them" or with addresses and messages that could be interpreted only by a certain clerk with "a wonderful knack in . . . deciphering atrocious penmanship." Twain's instructions to Bliss were, "use as many as you think proper."[6] Williams made ten drawings—mostly of envelopes—in keeping with the promise Twain made in his story: "I here offer them [the letters] for the inspection of the curious reader"[7] (Figs. 6 & 7).

The frog for the famous "Celebrated Jumping Frog" was to be a most important drawing. Ever since Webb's "gold-stamped" design on the cover of the first small book, Twain had wanted a "fully illustrated" version of his now well-known story.[8] His desire saw early fulfillment in a paper-covered sketch book, *Sketches* #1, which had been proposed by Twain in 1874 as the first in a possible series of pamphlets. *Sketches* #1 contained a "slightly revised version of the author's most famous sketch, illustrated by R. T. Sperry, who also produced the cover design: a cigar-smoking frog sitting underneath a toadstool, contemplating an edition of *Mark Twain's Sketches*"[9] (Fig. 8).

Nothing is known of the artist Sperry and little of the

abortive edition—there would be only one issue, and it had an ignominious end. The pamphlets with the cigar-smoking frog were ultimately sold to the Aetna Life Insurance Company to be used as part of an advertisement.[10] This blatantly commercial dumping of the unsold booklets for advertising apparently was carried out with Mark Twain's blessing.

In 1875 the frog sketch was once more proposed for illustration in the new book, *Sketches, New & Old*. True Williams was the artist, and it is worth noting that he was clever enough to make the frog, Daniel Webster, resemble the politician after whom he was named.

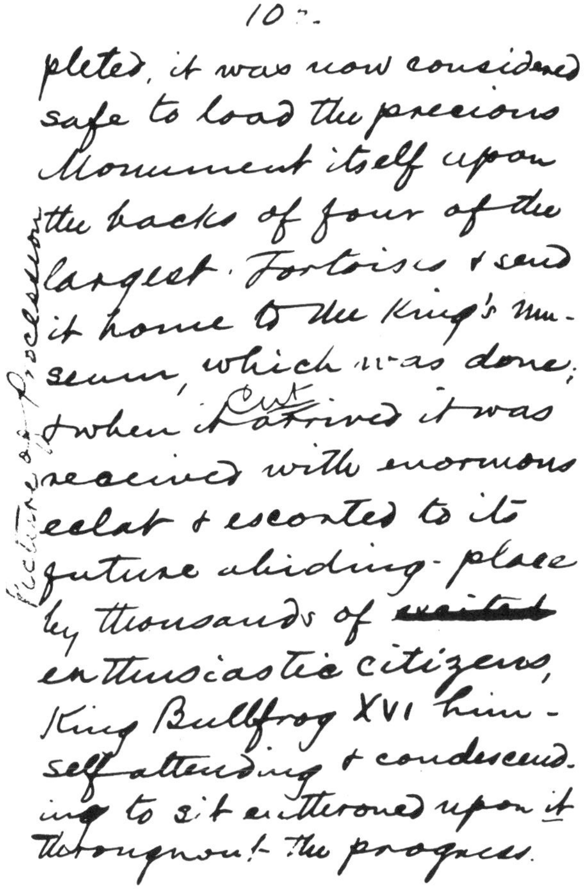
10 -.
pleted, it was now considered
safe to load the precious
Monument itself upon
the backs of four of the
largest Tortoises & send
it home to the King's mu-
seum, which was done;
& when it arrived it was
received with enormous
eclat & escorted to its
future abiding-place
by thousands of ~~excited~~
enthusiastic citizens,
King Bullfrog XVI him-
self attending & condescend-
ing to sit enthroned upon it
throughout the progress.

Fig. 2. Clemens' Manuscript, "Some Learned Fables."

Fig. 3. "Some Learned Fables," *Sketches, New & Old.*

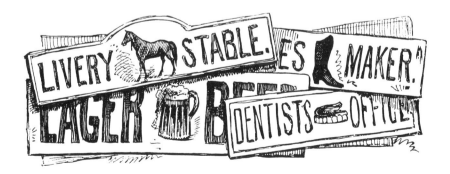

Fig. 4. "Some Learned Fables," *Sketches, New & Old.*

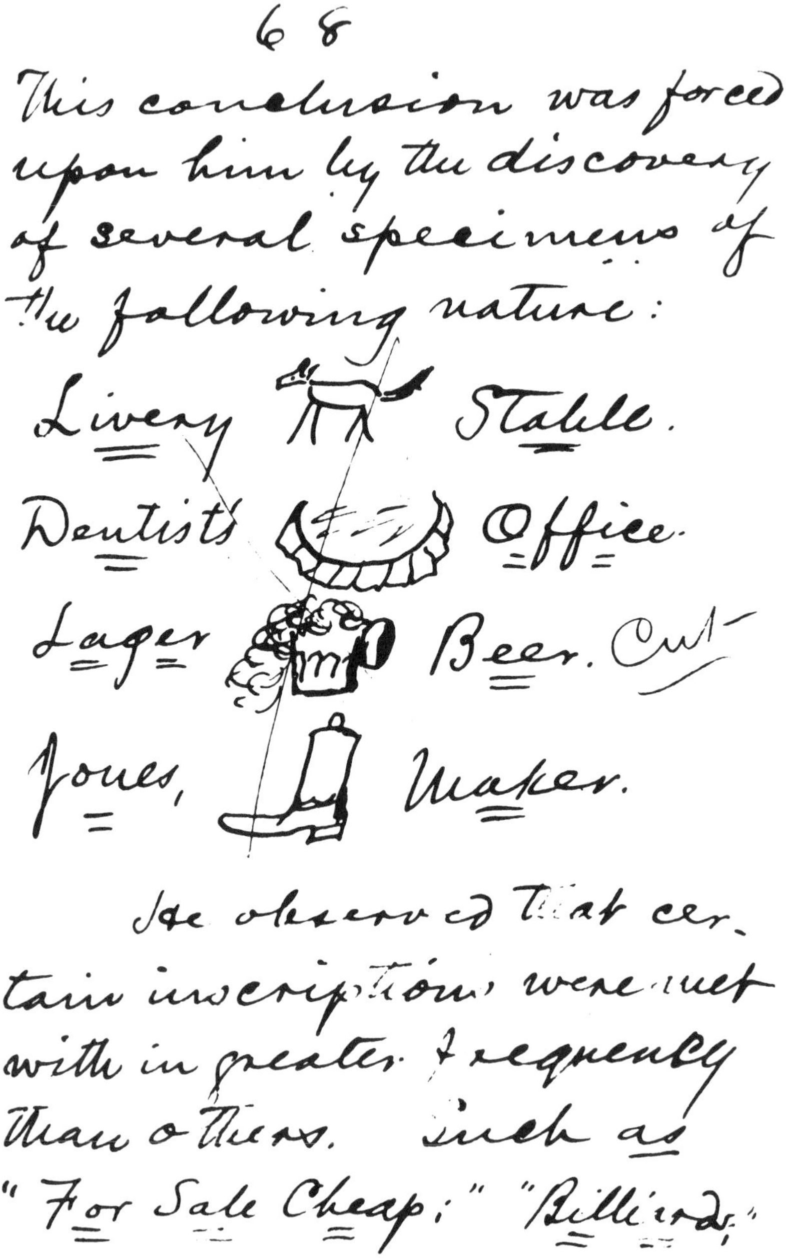

68

This conclusion was forced
upon him by the discovery
of several specimens of
the following nature:

Livery   Stable.

Dentist's   Office.

Lager   Beer. Cut-

Jones,   Maker.

He observed that cer-
tain inscriptions were met
with in greater frequency
than others. Such as
"For Sale Cheap;" "Billiards,"

Fig. 5. Clemens' Manuscript, "Some Learned Fables."

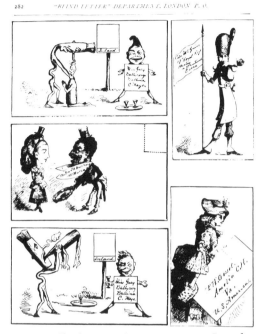

Fig. 6. "The 'Blind Letter' Department, London, P. O."

280 MARK TWAIN'S SKETCHES.

the most astonishing specimens he comes across. He also keeps fac-similes of many of the envelopes that pass through the office with queer pictures drawn

upon them. He was kind enough to have some of the picture-envelopes and

[TO THE MAJESTY THE QUEEN, AND THE PRINCESS OF WALES.]

execrable superscriptions copied for me, (the latter with "translations" added,) and I here offer them for the inspection of the curious reader.

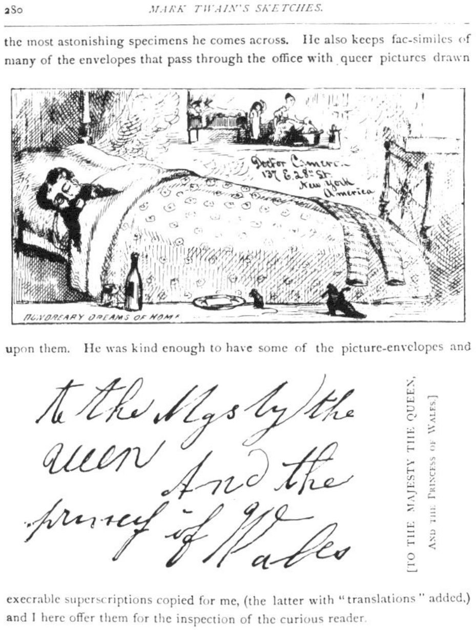

Fig. 7. "The 'Blind Letter' Department, London, P. O."

Fig. 8. Cover, *Sketches* #1, May-June 1874.

Fig. 9. DANIEL WEBSTER, "The Celebrated Jumping Frog."

It wasn't until years later that this resemblance was noted in print (Fig. 9):

> In 1907 William Lyon Phelps noted the appropriateness
> of naming the frog "Daniel Webster" and suggested that
> "the intense gravity of a frog's face, with the droop
> at the corners of the mouth, might well be envied by an
> American Senator."[11]

Mark Twain had remained in Hartford most of the summer of 1875 to consult with Williams and Bliss personally rather than by letter. Consequently, no documentary evidence exists of other Twain suggestions or of any influence he may have had on the illustration of *Sketches, New & Old*. It is known, however, that the illustrating process caused the usual publication delays and that Twain, despite the numerous postponements, eagerly awaited a spectacular design package for his new work.[12] The author and his readers were again disappointed. Bliss had assured would-be buyers of the book's artistic merits, with notices of the "sparkling humor of the Pen or Pencil." He had emphasized its "super-calendered, delicate tinted paper," and its "fanciful designs."[13] In reality the volume was inferior in paper, typography, and illustration.[14] Sales were light and Mark Twain soon realized that the book was not what he had hoped it would be. He also realized that part of the blame for the book's shortcomings must rest on his own shoulders. In a September letter to Howells, Twain mused: "I destroyed a mass of sketches, & now heartily wish I had destroyed some more of them."[15]

Sketches, New & Old had little chance for success. Its design was unattractive, even when compared with many other subscription books. Moreover, it ran counter to the subscription market tradition in at least two important ways: it included much previously-published material, and it relied heavily on the short story or the brief humorous fiction piece. There was little for the hard-headed subscription-book readers to get their teeth into. Unfortunately, Mark Twain and the American Publishing Company failed to recognize the problems or to learn from this lesson. Unwisely they decided to copy the format of *Sketches, New & Old* for Twain's next book, *The Adventures of Tom Sawyer*.

A comparison of first editions of these two books reveals remarkable similarities. Both volumes had fewer pages than the usual subscription work; and each had a high proportion of illustration: 320 pages and 130 drawings for *Sketches*; 275 pages and 161 drawings for *Tom Sawyer*. Both covers were blue with gold and black embossed designs.[16] Even the various characters

STORY OF THE BAD LITTLE BOY.

ONCE there was a bad little boy whose name was Jim—though, if you will notice, you will find that bad little boys are nearly always called James in your Sunday-school books. It was strange, but still it was true that this one was called Jim.

He didn't have any sick mother either—a sick mother who was pious and had the consumption, and would be glad to lie down in the grave and be at rest but for the strong love she bore her boy, and the anxiety she felt that the world might be harsh and cold towards him when she was gone. Most bad boys in the Sunday-books are named James, and have sick mothers,

TOM SAWYER. *The Adventures of Tom Sawyer.* Fig. 11.

JIM. "The Story of the Bad Little Boy." Fig. 10.

"HUCK" TRANSFORMED.
*The Adventures of Tom
Sawyer.* Fig. 13.

JACOB BLEVINS. "The Story
of a Good Little
Boy." Fig. 12.

CHAPTER XIX.

HISTORY REPEATS ITSELF.

THE following I find in a
Sandwich Island paper which
some friend has sent me from
that tranquil far-off retreat. The
coincidence between my own experience and that here set down
by the late Mr. Benton is so remarkable that I cannot forbear
publishing and commenting upon
the paragraph. The Sandwich
Island paper says:—

"How touching is this tribute of the late
Hon. T. H. Benton to his mother's influence:— 'My mother asked me never to
use tobacco; I have never touched it from
that time to the present day. She asked
me not to gamble, and I have never gam-
bled. I cannot tell who is losing in games
that are being played. She admonished
me, too, against liquor-drinking, and whatever capacity for endurance I have at
present, and whatever usefulness I may
have attained through life, I attribute to
having complied with her pious and correct wishes. When I was seven years of
age she asked me not to drink, and then
I made a resolution of total abstinence;
and that I have adhered to it through all
time I owe to my mother.'"

I never saw anything so curious. It is almost an exact epitome of my own
moral career—after simply substituting a grandmother for a mother. How
well I remember my grandmother's asking me not to use tobacco, good
old soul! She said, "You're at it again, are you, you whelp? Now, don't
ever let me catch you chewing tobacco before breakfast again, or I lay I'll black-
snake you within an inch of your life!" I have never touched it at that hour
of the morning from that time to the present day.

AUNT POLLY. *The Adventures
of Tom Sawyer.* Fig. 15.

GRANDMOTHER. "History
Repeats Itself." Fig. 14.

depicted by Williams could be (and were) transferred conveniently from the *Sketches* to *Tom Sawyer*: Jim in "The Story of the
Bad Little Boy" became Tom (Figs. 10 & 11); Jacob Blevins of
"The Story of a Good Little Boy" became Huck Finn (Figs. 12
& 13); and grandmother from a sketch entitled "History Repeats
Itself" became Aunt Polly (Figs. 14 & 15).[17] Since Williams had
been working on the two books almost concurrently, it probably
seemed eminently practical to all involved to merely slide the
design concepts from one work to another.

    This new Mark Twain book was another novel—not a
successful genre in the door-to-door market. Twain fleetingly
thought of taking his newest creation to a trade firm. But Bliss
had still another hold on him. The author had borrowed $2000
from the company to send his friend and fellow correspondent,
James Riley, to South Africa scouting material for a book on the
diamond mines there. Twain was planning to ghost-write Riley's
experiences to produce another six-hundred-page travel book.
Riley made the return trip, but unfortunately died of mouth
cancer in September 1872, before he and Mark Twain could exchange information. Since his debt to Bliss remained unpaid,
Twain once more calmly accepted the inevitable—the publication
of *Tom Sawyer* by the American Publishing Company.

    By early November Mark Twain was turning over manu-
script pages to Bliss. Both publisher and author agreed, without
debate or alternate considerations as far as can be discerned now,
that Williams should be the illustrator. Twain instructed Bliss to
give the manuscript to Williams:

> You may let Williams have all of Tom Sawyer that you
> have received. He can of course make the pictures all
> the more understandingly after reading the whole story.
> He wants it, and I have not the least objection, because
> if he should lose any of it I have got another complete
> MS. copy.[18]

Although it was Mark Twain who wrote both of Williams' desire
for the commission and of the handing over of manuscript to
start the sketches, there is no reason to suppose that either Bliss
or Twain objected to Williams as artist for the book. And
Williams would naturally want the assignment since he could
handle this commission with relative ease. His drawings for
Sketches, New & Old provided ready-made designs, and the pub-

lisher and author had decided the format would be the same as for the sketch book.

As Bliss received manuscript in the Hartford office he went through it and made recommendations in the margins for Williams' illustrations. Surprisingly, most of these ideas were ignored by the artist. For this project Williams took his own lead, making decisions on subject matter and the placement of various cuts.

One of Williams' concepts, a carry-over from *Sketches,* was an expansion of chapter-heading designs. More than the usual embellished letters, this time each chapter's first page contained an elaborate chapter number, an over-size and ornate first word (worked in as an integral part of the heading), and a full-size, inserted cut or vignette. These head pieces occupied from fifty to sixty per cent of the total page space—a practical approach since the text of *Tom Sawyer* badly needed bulk in order to please the subscription public. The concept created a problem, however, for the compositors. The head pieces had to be drawn, engraved, and ready *before* typesetting in order that the initial line measurement could be worked out. Since the engravers would again prove uncooperative at their stage in the assembly process, the many-staged production caused considerable confusion and delay.[19]

Only two of the head pieces, both early in the story, had marginal ideas penciled in, neither identifiable as the handwriting of Bliss or Twain:

> The first, on MS p. 23, pertains to chapter 2: "(Head cut Tom with whitewash pail at fence etc)"; the second, on MS p. 42, reads: "cut for head of chap. 3". But in the book the headcut for chapter 2 was an illustration of a figure carrying a pail captioned "JIM" [Fig. 16]; the headcut for chapter 3 was an illustration of a girl captioned "BECKY THATCHER" [Fig. 17] whereas the recommendation on MS p. 42 was opposite the passage where Aunt Polly expresses her pleasure after the whitewashing.[20]

So much for suggestions.

Unlike the unique head pieces, the tail pieces for *Tom Sawyer* adhered to the usual subscription formula. This was due both to coincidence and design. Fourteen of the thirty-five chapters are without tail pieces, since they end at or near the bottom of a page. Only two of the cuts are listed in the "List of Illustrations" as TAIL-PIECE. Three of the remaining nineteen cuts resemble stock cuts.[21] Only two of these tail pieces, as far as can be demonstrated now, were from available plates in Bliss's company: Peter, the cat, page 112, had appeared originally as Dick Baker's cat (Tom Quartz) in *Roughing It;* and YOUTH, page 41, which would appear later as a tail piece for *A Tramp*

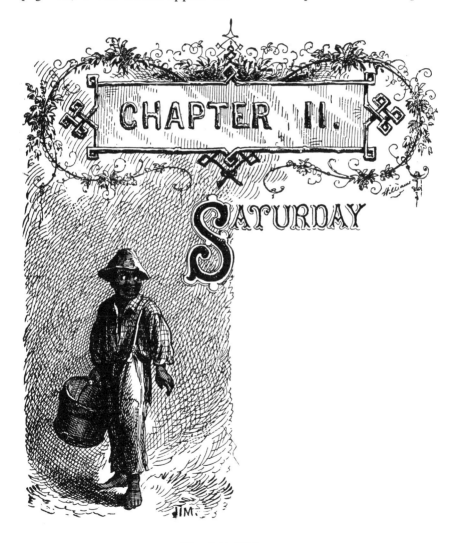

Fig. 16. JIM.

Fig. 17. BECKY THATCHER.

AFTER AN EXCURSION.

Fig. 18. AFTER AN EXCURSION. *Roughing It.*

Fig. 19. YOUTH.

Abroad (Figs. 18 & 19).[22]   The most bibliographically interesting tail piece in *Tom Sawyer*, however, was inserted in the last
page of the book.

True Williams is credited with drawing all the prints in the
book; most are signed by him, and his style is generally recognizable in the others. There is, however, one notable exception:
the tail piece on the last page of the book—presumably a picture
of Aunt Polly—is not in the Williams style. The image of this
last tail piece has a tangled history.

Most of Williams' renditions of Aunt Polly were copies of
ideas from the grandmother in *Sketches, New & Old*, as previously shown. But in this cut there is a difference. To trace
this Aunt Polly from its inception, it is necessary to follow a
sequence of drawings of a different woman, a Mrs. Partington.
An original pencil drawing of Mrs. Partington was done by
Josiah Wolcott for the *Boston Pathfinder* (Fig. 20). After his
stint on the *Pathfinder,* Wolcott took a turn as a contributing
illustrator for the *Carpet-Bag*, a weekly published in Boston
and edited by the creator of Mrs. Partington, B. P. Shillaber.
Thereafter, in each issue of the *Carpet-Bag*, there appeared a
small version of Wolcott's original *Pathfinder* Mrs. Partington,
as a head piece. In this cut there was also incorporated an
additional character—a young boy stealing a lump of sugar
(Fig. 21). In issue No. 13 of the weekly, Wolcott's original
portrait of the lady appeared twice—once as the usual head
piece, and again (much enlarged) as an illustration in the body
of the publication (Fig. 22).

Benjamin Penhallow Shillaber had produced short stories
about Mrs. Partington for the *Carpet-Bag* and in 1854 he published a book about the old lady's conversations. Curiously,
Shillaber did not commission Wolcott to work his now familiar
Mrs. Partington into the pages of the *Carpet-Bag*. He hired a
Frederick M. Coffin instead. Thirty-two-year-old Coffin was
just beginning his illustrating career. Making up for lost time,
Coffin was ambitiously producing drawings for at least ten books
in the same year he worked for Shillaber. Furiously sketching
everything from dogs to landscapes, Coffin expediently copied
Wolcott's illustration of Mrs. Partington from No. 13 of the
Carpet-Bag to use as a frontispiece for his Shillaber book. This
was, of course, a time-saving measure, but it was also an effective
eye-catching device, since the image of Wolcott's Mrs. Partington
was firmly planted in most readers' minds from her frequent

appearance in the Shillaber journal. Sinclair Hamilton, illustrated-book collector and writer from Princeton, has traced the history of the Aunt Polly image.

MRS. RUTH PARTINGTON. Josiah Wolcott, Pencil Drawing.
Fig. 20.

Fig. 21. *The Carpet-Bag.*

MRS. RUTH PARTINGTON, RELICT OF CORPORAL PAUL PARTINGTON, U.S.A.

Fig. 22. MRS. RUTH PARTINGTON, RELICT OF CORPORAL
PAUL PARTINGTON, U. S. A. Josiah Wolcott, *The Carpet-Bag.*
Vol. I, No. 13, 1851.

> For the book it [Wolcott's picture] was redrawn . . .
> [and] minor differences are apparent. In the book
> there is far more shading, the teapot and the snuff box
> are smaller and so is the cup which no longer is partly
> concealed by Mrs. Partington's shoulder, while the design
> of the Constitution and Guerriere on the handkerchief
> in Mrs. Partington's lap, cherished relict of Corporal
> Partington, her deceased mate, is now no longer dis-
> tinguishable. But the general design and, in particular,
> Mrs. Partington's "liniments" are substantially the same,
> and Coffin, in other illustrations in the book depicting
> Mrs. Partington, has made her conform to Wolcott's
> portrait of her.[23]

Williams' Aunt Polly, in the tail piece for *The Adventures of Tom
Sawyer,* was a redrawing (though anything but a photographic
reproduction) of the Wolcott-Coffin Mrs. Partington. The caption, of course, was changed—not to AUNT POLLY but simply
CONTENTMENT (Fig. 23). Again, from Hamilton:

> The portrait of Aunt Polly at p. 274 of *The Adventures
> of Tom Sawyer* . . . is an exact [sic] reproduction of the
> frontispiece in *The Life and Sayings of Mrs. Partington.*
> Either the original block was used or a photo-mechanical
> reproduction made. . . . Twain, consciously or uncon-
> sciously, fashioned his Aunt Polly after Mrs. Partington....
> It is not surprising, therefore, that Wolcott's [Coffin's]
> drawing of Mrs. Partington should have been used for
> Aunt Polly.[24]

The ticklish question, so far as this study is concerned, is
not who drew the original image or how many times it had been
copied before it was used in *Tom Sawyer,* but rather who
decided to place the Wolcott-Coffin print on the next-to-last page
of Mark Twain's book.[25] There are many possible culprits. Bliss
may have found the print in the Shillaber book and had it
photographically reproduced. It is unlikely that Bliss had a
previously engraved plate on hand since the Shillaber book was
published in New York in 1854 by J. C. Derby. When Bliss
borrowed plates, he usually favored those from a current year
and from his own firm. Bliss, however, is not the most obvious
suspect.

It is more probable that Mark Twain and True Williams

teamed up in some way to transfer the image from Shillaber's book to Twain's. It is known that Twain was in contact with

Fig. 23. CONTENTMENT. *The Adventures of Tom Sawyer.*

Williams during the months the illustrator sketched the *Tom Sawyer* drawings. A Bliss letter of the summer chastises Mark Twain for confiding in the artist: "Even the poor drunken Williams comes and boastingly taunts me with what you tell him."[26]

Moreover, Twain, not Bliss or Williams, was the one person most aware of the heavy debt he owed to Shillaber's Mrs. Partington. Mark Twain's description in his novel has since often been cited by scholars as having been borrowed from B. P. Shillaber's *The Life and Sayings of Mrs. Partington*. Twain may even have given Williams the Shillaber book with the print of the woman to use as a guide. Williams had also borrowed a silhouette outline of Corporal Partington—which had been background material in the Coffin picture—for a Chapter X tail piece (Fig. 24). Therefore it seems probable that Williams had the book and was amenable to the copying scheme that could save him time. Team work between Williams and Twain seems the most plausible answer for how the Wolcott-Coffin picture could have slipped into the last pages of *Tom Sawyer*.[27]

The joke on the public would appeal to Williams, who had a whimsical though perverse sense of humor. In one other cut for *Tom Sawyer* he engraved his own name on one of the tombstones in the Muff Potter graveyard scene. Words etched on the stone read: SACRED TO THE MEMORY OF T. W. WILLIAMS[28] (Fig. 25).

Though little evidence remains of Mark Twain's part in getting that final tail piece into *Tom Sawyer*, there is no doubt that he was at least partly (and perhaps solely) responsible for two illustrations in the book. In the right-hand margin of his manuscript page describing Tom's drawing of a "dismal caricature of a house," Twain had marginally noted "Picture of house." There is more than a possibility that "he [Twain] himself drew the illustration, for it was in the style and within the range of his talent."[29] Significant in evidence for this claim is the fact that the author had already tried preliminary sketches in the *Enterprise* and in *Sketches, New & Old*; and would, within a few years, supply a number of original drawings for *A Tramp Abroad* (Fig. 26). Another piece of "art work"—though not, strictly speaking, an illustration—for which the author is responsible in this book is the longhand version of Tom's oath, which Twain undoubtedly drafted and sent on as a final print (Fig. 27):

Fig. 24. TOM TALKS WITH HIS AUNT.

INJUN JOE'S TWO VICTIMS.

Fig. 25. INJUN JOE'S TWO VICTIMS.

TOM AS AN ARTIST.

Fig. 26. TOM AS AN ARTIST.

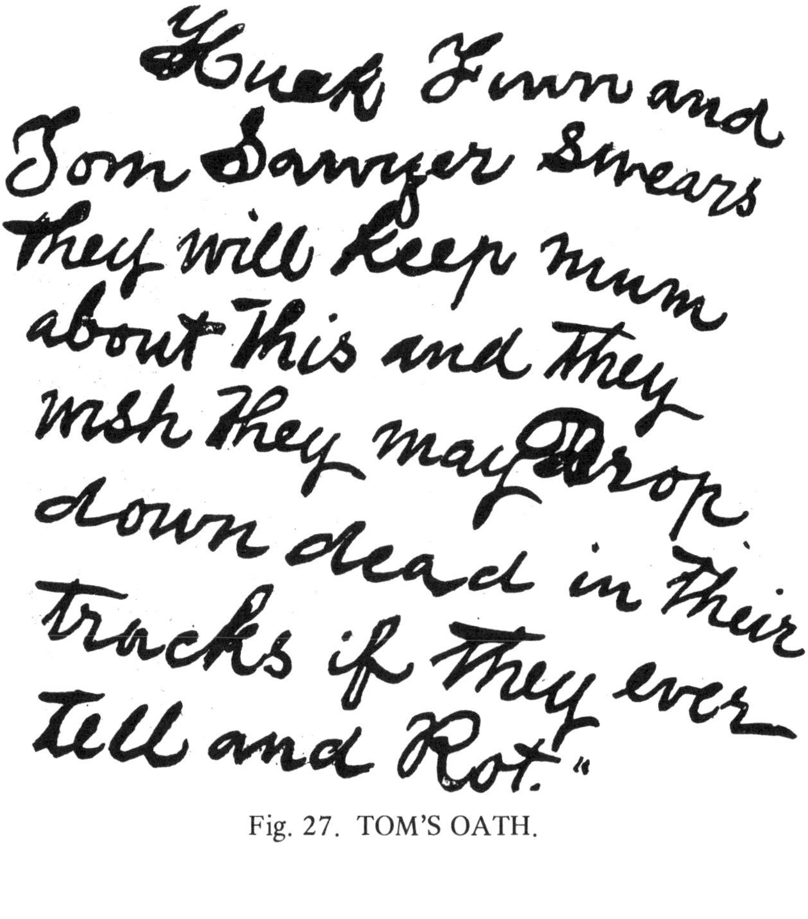

Huck Finn and Tom Sawyer Swears they will keep mum about This and They wish They may Drop down dead in Their tracks if They ever tell and Rot."

Fig. 27. TOM'S OATH.

> At the bottom of MS p. 260 Mark Twain wrote and canceled the first two lines of the "oath". He probably wrote it in full on MS p. 261, from which a cut was then made, for MS p. 261 survives only as a small portion of a half-sheet. The missing portion of MS p. 261 probably contained a marginal note indicating cut 35.[30]

Clemens bypassed most of the editorial decisions for the American edition. His attention during the manufacturing process of *Tom Sawyer* was with copyright problems and the continuing poor quality of his English editions. From the time of his earliest publication abroad, all of his books had been pirated, and only one of the foreign editions had been fully illustrated. In the middle 1870's, to protect himself from further abuse, Twain began a crusade to strengthen international copyright laws. He wrote an essay entitled "Petition for International Copyright" in 1875. (His brief and pointed "Petition Concerning Copyright" had appeared in *Sketches, New & Old*.) Working through his English publishers he now began a campaign to implement his ideas with a view to protecting *Tom Sawyer*.

As a first step toward establishing control over his copyright here and abroad, Clemens cautiously asked Bliss if he had made any previous arrangements with British publishers:

> What have you heard from England in the way of a proposition for Tom Sawyer? I have an offer from the Routledges (which I haven't answered), and if you have heard nothing from over there, I propose to write the "Temple Bar" people.[31]

Bliss had neglected to contact editors abroad. Clemens quickly shelved his idea of writing the Temple Bar publishers and instead contacted an old acquaintance, Dr. Moncure Daniel Conway.

Conway was an American living and working in the British Isles. On an extended lecture tour of the States, he had gotten together with Clemens to discuss a special Conway plan for the publication of books in England. The more Clemens reviewed the idea the more intrigued he became. He wrote inviting Conway to Hartford to talk about the feasibility of the scheme. After the visit he again wrote Conway, instructing him to begin the process:

> I want you to take my new book to England, & have it

published there by some one (according to your plan) before it is issued here, if you will be so good.[32]

A willing Conway wrote the details to his wife in Britian, asking her to negotiate with the English firm of Chatto and Windus:

> He (Mark T.) would like to follow our plan—pay for the manufacture of his own book and pay the publisher for each copy sold. . . . You can also inform Chatto that the story is very important & illustrated with 150 engravings, & that plates can be sent over at once for the early May publication. . . . I shall bring the Manuscript (of which two copies exist) with me. It is probable that two editions will have to be issued, one cheap.[33]

A "cheap" edition was to prove a commercial blunder. However, at this early stage, Chatto and Windus were delighted with the opportunity to publish one of America's best-known humorists. They accepted Conway's idea, writing in their response:

> We shall be happy to undertake the publication of Mark Twain's new work upon the terms suggested by you. . . . —viz. that he should bear the entire cost of production, and pay us a royalty of 10 per cent upon the entire amount of sales.[34]

Since Clemens had long been determined to produce his own book, and reap what he thought would be the substantial profits from such an arrangement, he was as enthralled as Chatto with the opportunity.

Conway returned to England and, as Clemens' agent, labored long and hard over final contracts. He pitted the offer from Chatto against a bid from Routledge, Clemens' former English publisher, weighing the merits of a commission deal (Clemens paying the production costs) against a straight royalty contract. Publishing by commission would entail Clemens' meeting not only the cost of manufacture but also the advertising bills—an estimated outlay of £ 500 immediately and £ 500 later.[35] Wisely Olivia intervened and talked her husband into settling for the royalty contract, persuading him that "it simplifies everything; removes all risk; requires no outlay of capital; . . . [and] a gain of 25 per cent profit is hardly worth the trouble and risk of publishing on your own account."[36] Poor cash flow and the liberal royalty offer from Chatto, as well as Olivia Clemens' good sense, settled the debate.

Clemens accepted the Chatto contract, which featured a sliding royalty scale with a top figure of twenty-five per cent on the most expensive edition. He turned a second manuscript copy of *Tom Sawyer* over to Andrew Chatto and left production details up to him and Conway.

Even before the English presses started there were trans-atlantic mails filled with shipping schedules and lists of electro-plate costs. The first complication centered on traditional American and British book sizes. Before contracts were signed Conway had warned Clemens:

> It will be positively necessary . . . for the book to appear here [England] in a difft shape from the American—(which here is fatally unorthodox). I sent you by book-post a copy of Tom Hood's Nowhere & North Pole as an indication of the kind of book we shall have to make here.[37]

The Tom Hood book that Conway sent Clemens measured 7 9/16 x 5 1/2"; smaller than the American subscription book which measured 8 5/16 x 6 9/16". The larger book correspond-ed to an English second-class "Picture Toy Book." Publishing in an oversize format would categorize an English *Tom Sawyer* as children's literature.

Clemens, confused, argued in ocean-hopping letters with Conway:

> We *borrowed* our shape and style of book *from England.* We exactly copied the size, style, and get-up. . . . But still, you and Chatto must freely do as you like. If you still do not want to make the book the size of ours and take a set of plates containing the cuts and everything, telegraph thus:
> "Twain—Hartford—pictures."
> I will then send any and all pictures that can be cut down to your size.—And send the original drawings of the rest.
> If you *should* take a notion to have full plates, just telegraph "Plates," instead of "Pictures." . . .
> Bliss can't give me price of full plates or pictures

either, yet—but says he will make it just as cheap as he possibly can.—for *me*.[38]

In the end Clemens and Conway agreed on the smaller size and Clemens began negotiating with Bliss on costs. Then ensued another apparent communications breakdown: Bliss originally had given Clemens a price for full-size electros and now thought he should review his cost figures for a new set of reduced-size pictures. Frank Bliss became the intermediary correspondent:

> Father says that he had an estimate all ready for the electros of "Tom Sawyer," but as you changed the size it involves making a new estimate all through, & he is fearful that reducing the size so much, of many of the cuts, will interfere with their printing nicely, he is making inquiries about it.[39]

Clemens immediately replied that he didn't want a new but only a revised estimate on the *original* set of plates that would fit into the English edition. Conway, for his part, pledged that he would supervise all the changes, that the work would "be done with artistic care so as not to impair the figures," and that he would revise all the proof "personally."[40] With an apparent agreement on procedure, Chatto set up the text pages and had the galley proofs ready, without illustration, by the first of May.

Meanwhile, back in the States, Williams had completed his part of the operation by early January. Clemens was well satisfied with the *Tom Sawyer* illustrations, as he wrote in a letter to Howells:

> Williams has made about 200 rattling pictures for it [*Tom Sawyer*]—some of them very dainty. Poor devil, what a genius he has, & how he does murder it with rum. He takes a book of mine, & without suggestion from anybody builds no end of pictures just from his reading of it.[41]

Though Williams had finished the original drawings by January and Clemens had examined them, the author realized that the British edition was likely to be ready well before the American. In a letter to Conway—in fact, the same letter in which he had discussed the size of the Chatto book—Clemens wrote: "We certainly cannot issue here before May 1st, if we can even do it then. Hardly any of the pictures are finished yet. I have read only 2 chapters in proof, and they had blanks for the cuts."[42] The engravers were, as usual, holding up completed proof. Clemens found out at the end of April that the *electrotypes* would certainly take another month.[43] By this time Howells had already written his review, having read the novel from the illustration-free proof. Clemens and Bliss realized that they had missed the spring market and agreed to postpone publication until fall—though Howells' review would appear in May. Clemens suggested that Chatto and Windus also postpone publication, but he somewhat casually gave them leave to publish whenever it seemed best to them. Conway and Chatto hastily wrote to Clemens, "We shall come out here just so soon as we can get hold of the electros of pictures which we are anxiously expecting."[44]

During this see-saw of letters Conway had been lecturing in London. His subject was Mark Twain's new book—specifically, the scene of Tom whitewashing the fence. The response from his English audiences was so enthusiastic that both Conway and Chatto decided to issue a cheap, unillustrated edition immediately. Since the electro problem was being tediously drawn out, they agreed to wait to publish an illustrated edition for Christmas. By then, they believed, the promised plates would have arrived. The unillustrated first volume was published 9 June 1876, six full months before the American edition. The British reviews were favorable and sales were brisk—although the English reader had a difficult time deciding whether the book was for young people or adults.

Even after the British publication, letters about the electros continued, Clemens writing to Bliss about plate shipments and to Conway about prices. At first Bliss stubbornly resisted but he finally shipped the plates. He then began a billing debate with Chatto. The issue became so heated that Clemens offered to personally split the costs of the plates with Chatto in order to settle the matter. After lengthy correspondence and final shipping of the electros, the British Christmas edition was issued in December without illustration, but in "illustrated boards." It was not until 1885 that a fully illustrated English edition, with True Williams' prints, was issued.[45]

The premature publication of the first unillustrated English edition caused critical complications for Mark Twain. A Canadian publisher, Belford Brothers, pirated the English version and

brought out a Canadian *Tom Sawyer* on 29 July 1876. A furious
Clemens wrote to Conway:

> [Belford is] flooding America with a cheap pirated
> edition of Tom Sawyer. . . . We cannot issue for 6 weeks
> yet, and by that time Belford will have sold 100,000
> over the frontier and killed my book dead. This piracy
> will cost me $10,000.[46]

Clemens' attempts to facilitate his English publication
through Conway had both profits and losses. On the plus side
the British editions were very successful financially and Clemens
had found a reputable publisher and a friend in Andrew Chatto.
On the minus side, the Canadian piracy had all but ruined the
American market. Clemens sued Belford, but the American
copyright law, which decreed that English copyright had no
bearing on Canadian rights, held in court. Clemens lost the
legal battle and the American sales. Copyright problems of this
nature continued to plague Clemens for many years to come.

Not all of Clemens' problems were legal. He had to personally accept part of the blame for the delay in the American
edition. The wrangle about page sizes, added to his concern
over English copyright *if* the American edition should precede
the English, had put an early crimp in the process. Later, when
he became convinced that spring was a poor time to promote
his book, he postponed publication and opted for an autumn
issue. These procrastinations only compounded the usual delays
caused by the illustrations. By September Clemens was attempting to shift the entire blame for the late issue. Writing to his
German publisher he fumed: "The American edition has been
delayed by the artists & engravers, & will not issue from the
press for two months yet."[47]

Although Williams was not a cause for the delay, he was
largely responsible—despite the flattering things Clemens said
of him in the letter to Conway quoted above—for the inferior
artistic quality of the designs in *Tom Sawyer*. The craftsmanship in the book was at its lowest level for American Publishing
Company editions. Williams' sketches had lost all the crispness
and intensity so evident in his work on other Mark Twain books.
An excessive use of cross-hatching gave to his new style a somber-
ness that was aggravated by the engravers' coarse lines and a
heavy inking of the plates. Scenes were dark, dull, and un-

interesting. Gone was the hard edge of good graphic design; all lines were smudged into a fog of greys. The paper was slick, a heavy quality gloss, but the printing was inferior. The pictures of Tom, Huck, Aunt Polly, Jim, and the rest were, for the most part, cardboard duplicates of the portraits in *Sketches, New & Old*. Beyond being shallow, they were also often inconsistent in characterization, though authentic in depicting the clothing of the times.

Williams' rendition of the mischievous Tom, introduced to the readers in the frontispiece of the first edition, may seem a bit "precious" to a current American audience. Historically, however, Tom and other persons from the novel are represented with amazing accuracy, dressed in the average garb of Upper Missourians in the late 1850's.

The frontispiece serves as an example of Williams' fastidiousness. We might now consider it an inconsistency that Tom should be in his bare feet while otherwise dressed in his Sunday best. (Throughout the novel Tom is persistently barefoot.) That seeming inconsistency virtually disappears, however, when one understands the make-up of the shoes of the era (Fig. 28).

> Shoes and boots were distinguished in several aspects but comfort was clearly not one of them. To begin with, they were undifferenced as to left and right . . . with soles attached by wooden pegs.[48]

No wonder Tom was frustrated when he had to wear shoes.

The trousers, then called "pantaloons," were ankle-length both in real life and in Williams' sketches, rolled up probably to escape the inevitable Missouri mud. The pants were usually of the broadfall type, much like a sailor's. The whole front let down and they were buttoned at the sides—though Williams neglects to add the button detailing. Pantaloons were held up by suspenders (duly depicted by Williams), often called "galluses" and usually made of fabric or leather.

Boys' shirts, when seen in the book, are consistent with the standard of the time: full-sleeved with tight-fitting cuffs; long-tailed—though Tom's shirt-tail does not show even when Williams has him walking on his hands to impress Becky Thatcher[49]—with buttons extending only about one-third of the way from neck to waist, so that access would have to be by an over-the-head maneuver; collarless, or with slightly rounded collar—Tom's shirt always has the rounded version.

> Over the shirt was worn a "roundabout" lapelled jacket of fustian or wool, coming just below the waist. Some buttoned all the way down like a waistcoat, but more fastened only at the top button, opening progressively wider as it descended.[50]

As to hats, it seems amazing that Tom is shown not only completely dressed but also hatted most of the time in the illustrations. Boys in the days of Tom Sawyer often wore a rounded version of a felt hat with a narrow brim.

Fig. 28. FRONTISPIECE, TOM SAWYER.

A fair approximation of the clothing of the time may be seen to-day in the consciously old-fashioned garments worn by the more conservative Amish Mennonite sects in the United States.

At Sunday School or on special occasions, boys added, usually under duress, a floppy tie—Byron fashion. But the Sunday and weekday attire were basically the same, the Sunday being the newer and larger (room-to-grow) version of the tight and threadbare weekday ensemble.

Williams' young ladies are as accurately portrayed as the young men. Becky wears, as was the style of the time, layers and layers of skirts. From under the layers, even when barefoot, "pantalettes," the demure feminine counterpart of pantaloons, are seen to be ruffled. The ruffles are subtly decorative, and the limbs are decorously covered. The girls' shirtwaists are utilitarian rather than fashionable or comfortable—though Williams takes license with Becky's dresses, making them un-usually dainty.

Huck is as accurately drawn as Tom. His attire is quite different from Tom's, but the differences are entirely in char-acter. That is to say, in costuming Huck, Williams took his cue from the text:

> Huckleberry was always dressed in the cast-off clothes
> of full-grown men. . . . His hat was a vast ruin with a
> wide crescent lopped out of its brim; his coat, when he
> wore one, hung nearly to his heels.[51]

The oversize coat that Williams gives Huck is appropriate; one of the signs of adulthood was the discarding of the short round-about in favor of a long sack or frock coat. Huck, therefore, wears the "cast-off" coat of an adult rather than the short jacket of the other boys in the novel (Fig. 29).

Although Mark Twain thought of Tom and Huck as being both the same age—twelve or thereabouts—Williams' Huck appears much older, perhaps because of his adult attire.[52] It is somewhat distracting, however, that both boys change as the reader leafs through the pages. Tom, as shown in the earlier chapters, tends to be the scolded, blond prankster, but in later illustrations he seems a semi-sophisticated adolescent. Huck, on the other hand, tends to switch from a pipe-smoking old man to a soft-faced, frightened child (Figs. 30, 31, & 32).

Williams may have been keenly aware of boys' attire, but he

often seems strangely unaware of boys themselves. This lack of
awareness is particularly evident in his handling of Jim. The

HUCKLEBERRY FINN.

Fig. 29. HUCKLEBERRY FINN.

HUCK AT HOME.

Fig. 30. HUCK AT HOME.

COMFORTABLE ONCE MORE.

Fig. 31. COMFORTABLE ONCE MORE.

NOT AMISS.

Fig. 32. NOT AMISS.

Fig. 33. OUT OF BONDAGE [Tom, Jim and Huck],
Adventures of Huckleberry Finn.

negro boy looks like something off a cut-plug tobacco label.
Negro boys must have been rare in Hartford, although, admittedly, young Jim as drawn by Williams was typical of the stereotype
of the black at this time. More realistic and honest portrayals of
Mark Twain's blacks would have to wait for E. W. Kemble's
drawings for *The Adventures of Huckleberry Finn* (Fig. 33).

Williams drew boys' clothes accurately enough, but he was
guilty of seriously misinterpreting some aspects of the novel.
His drawings of Injun Joe, for example, are anything but
satisfactory. He seems to have made little attempt to give this
character consistently recognizable Indian features. And he
comes far short of doing justice to Injun Joe's disguise when Joe
returns to the village as "the old deaf and dumb Spaniard."[53]
The long-haired, bewhiskered "Spaniard," his eyes hidden behind
green goggles (Fig. 34), is simply too well disguised, as is the man
stretched out on the floor in "the haunted room" (Fig. 35)
—Injun Joe in a drunken slumber, looking as if he might awaken
shortly and ask Tom why he is trembling. Williams, however, is
perhaps less to be blamed than Mark Twain for the inconsistent
and unconvincing drawings of Injun Joe. Twain himself is vague
about Joe's appearance, especially in the Spanish disguise. The
green goggles appear to have been forgotten after Twain's first
mention of them. And there is nothing to indicate whether the
eye-patch—mentioned twice by the author and ignored by
Williams—is a protective device needed by Injun Joe or merely
a part of the disguise.

Fig. 34. INJUN JOE.

THE HAUNTED ROOM.

Fig. 35. THE HAUNTED ROOM.

It has been argued that True Williams blundered, too, in depicting the now famous whitewashing scene. Warren Chappell has this to say of the blunder:

> Williams did not always take care in reading the text. As the first man to do the whitewashing scene, he carelessly used a rail fence instead of a board fence which is described. For pictorial reasons, he might have cut down on the "thirty yards of board fence, nine feet high," but his measly rail fence is not suited to shielding Tom's actions from Aunt Polly in the ensuing scene.[54]

However, it needs to be pointed out that Mark Twain himself seemed undecided about the fence's size—if not its makeup. In the original manuscript used by Williams, Twain's fence measured four feet high, although this size was at some point canceled with strike marks on the page (Figs. 36 & 37).[55]   It is hard to say where the blame lies, but one thing seems certain: better communication between author and artist would have made for a more authentic representation of Injun Joe, the whitewashed fence, and a good many other characters and incidents in *Tom Sawyer*.

Fig. 36. Tom Sawyer's Fence, Hannibal, Missouri.

‘ AIN'T THAT WORK ?

Fig. 37. "AIN'T THAT WORK?"

Williams' haphazard, casual attitude about facts, the mere duplication of characters from *Sketches, New & Old,* and the dull and dark cross-hatching in the designs, dampened the spirit of Mark Twain's tale.   Unfortunately, as Warren Chappell points out, the flaws in Williams' original drawings are compounded by the work of unskilled engravers:

> Those illustrations which are handled tonally are en-
> graved in a most mechanical and matter-of-fact way.
> . . . As the book is leafed through, the illustrations
> seem to lack the humor that pervades the text.[56]

Mark Twain was apparently as little interested in offering suggestions (and as careless in reading proof) as Williams and the engravers were in their share of the production—partly, no doubt, because his attention was too much on problems of copyright, foreign publication, and literary piracy. He had not yet learned that he must exercise full control over both his manuscript and the complicated process of illustrating a book.

And he paid heavily for dividing his attention in this way; for he lost the copyright battle, and the overall design of *Tom Sawyer* shows the marks of his neglect. The marvel is that notwithstanding the flaws attributable to author, artist, engraver, publisher, and others, *Tom Sawyer* became and remains one of the classics of our literature.

After the publication of *Tom Sawyer,* Clemens' concerns were instantly directed to the poor market rather than the poor workmanship. Bliss's early predictions about publishing a sketchbook of "old" material and his words that "novels did poorly in the subscription market" proved tellingly prophetic for both *Sketches, New & Old* and *Tom Sawyer.*

The reviews were of little help in selling *Tom Sawyer*. Most of the promotion for the novel had been scheduled too early. Indeed Howells' review, as well as the English reviews, appeared a full six months before the American edition was issued. At the time of American publication few other reviewers even bothered to comment on the book. One of the critics in the *New York Times* praised the characterization of Tom, Aunt Polly, and more particularly Huck, but called it a *clever child's book* [italics mine], and then went on to condemn the violence in both the writing and the illustrations. The reviewer wrote of the "ugly murder in the book, over-minutely described and too fully illustrated," concluding that *Tom Sawyer* would have been a more attractive book if the author had given us "less . . . of Injun Joe and 'revenge,' and 'slitting women's ears,' and the shadow of the gallows."[57]

As a result of the bad timing, the bad promotion, the lukewarm reviews, and the not-very-imaginative illustrating, early American sales of *Tom Sawyer* were disappointing—23,638. In fact by the end of 1879, profits from *The Adventures of Tom Sawyer* and *Sketches, New & Old* combined brought Clemens only $15,000. In view of these figures—disastrous figures when compared with those for, say, *The Innocents Abroad*—the death knell was sounding for the relationship between Samuel Clemens and his publisher, Elisha Bliss.

Notes

[1]According to DeLancey Ferguson, "The Petrified Truth," *Colophon*, n. s. 11 (Winter 1939), 189-96, "Search has turned up no truth to support MT's claim that many were taken in by his Nevada 'petrified man' hoax." Later scholars, however, verify Clemens' claim that, "of the twelve California and Nevada papers that are known to have reprinted 'Petrified Man,' eight of them gave no sign whatever that they doubted the truth of the story" (*ET&S*, 1, 158).

[2]*ET&S*, 1, 641. The illustration appears on page 239 of the first edition.

[3]*ET&S*, 1, 159.

[4]Mark Twain, *Sketches, New & Old* (Hartford: The American Publishing Company, 1875), p. 241. Hereafter cited as *SkNO*.

[5]*ET&S*, 1, 641-642. Clemens' "picture of procession" appears on page 126 of the first edition.

[6]*ET&S*, 1, 620. Printer's copy at Yale. Clemens also suggested the copying of his famous fortification of Paris map: "Use an *accurate facsimile* of this map, with all its studied imperfections" (*ET&S*, 1, 620). The map, however, was never included in *Sketches, New & Old*.

[7]*SkNO*, pp. 280-282.

[8]"I think of a Jumping Frog *pamphlet* (illustrated) for next Christmas" (SLC to EB, 22 December 1870, *CL2*); see also *ET&S*, 1, 611.

[9]*ET&S*, 1, 611.

[10]*ET&S*, *1*, 616-617, and note 181.

[11]Documents, 1876 MTP. Authenticated by Irving S. Underhill, 2 May 1926. William Lyon Phelps, "Mark Twain," *North American Review* (July 1907), 540-548. Williams designed as a gift for Clemens and sent to him a "Jumping Frog New Year's Card of 1876."

[12]"Dan De Quille (who was visiting the author at Hartford) wrote his sister that 'Mark is getting out a book. . . . His "frog" and other old sketches . . . will be handsomely illustrated' " (*ET&S*, 1, 622). "I think it [*SkNO*] is an exceedingly handsome book" (SLC to Howells, 14 September 1875, *MTHL*, I:99).

[13]*MT&EB*, pp. 97-98.

[14]*ET&S*, 1, 645; also see critique in *MT&EB*, p. 97.

[15]*MTHL*, I:99.

[16] According to *BMT*, p. 24, "The cover, but for the lettering, is an almost exact duplicate of the *Tom Sawyer* binding."

[17] Illustrations appear in these first editions: p. 51 of *SkNO* and p. 42 of *Tom Sawyer*; p. 60 of *SkNO* and p. 268 of *Tom Sawyer*; and p. 271 of *SkNO* and p. 158 of *Tom Sawyer*.

[18] SLC to EB, 5 November [1875], *MTLP*, p. 92. Williams worked on cuts for *Tom Sawyer* between 5 November 1875 and 18 January 1876, (*The Works of Mark Twain: The Adventures of Tom Sawyer, Tom Sawyer Abroad, Tom Sawyer Detective*, ed. John C. Gerber, Paul Baender, and Terry Firkins [Berkeley, Los Angeles, London: University of California Press], p. 509, note 6). Hereafter cited as *Works: Tom Sawyer*.

[19] Problems with the head pieces discussed in *Works: Tom Sawyer*, pp. 524-526, item 135.32. According to Charles Norton, *Writing Tom Sawyer: The Adventures of a Classic* (Jefferson, North Carolina: McFarland & Company, Inc., 1983), p. 88, "The extra chapter in the English edition ('XVI') was probably a correct rendering of Twain's original wishes, the difference being an error made later on the part of True Williams. The illustrator of the American edition misread the original manuscript numbering, which he used when sketching his illustrations for the head of each chapter, these being drawings incorporating the chapter numbers. This mistake allowed two chapters to be run together, an error the author discovered while checking the final proof sheets, but considered not worth the trouble to correct." Hereafter cited as Norton, *Writing Tom Sawyer*.

[20] *Works: Tom Sawyer*, p. 508, note 5.

[21] Stock cuts include: THE PINCH BUG, p. 59; IN THE COILS (also in *TGA*), p. 126; TAIL PIECE, p. 263. *Works: Tom Sawyer* cites tail piece on page 263 as an example of parallels in headgear between the American and English editions (p. 509, note 6). The disputed caps were probably all drawn by Williams since this cap design was copied by him from ideas in *SkNO*.

[22] *BMT*, p. 29. Illustrations: uncaptioned tail piece but in the "List of Illustrations" as DEMORALIZED, in *Tom Sawyer* first edition, p. 112; uncaptioned tail piece in *Roughing It*, first edition, p. 442; uncaptioned tail piece but in the "List of Illustrations" as YOUTH, in *Tom Sawyer* first edition, p. 41; TAIL PIECE, in *A Tramp Abroad* first edition, p. 89.

[23] Hamilton, II, 152. Discussion on Aunt Polly's lineage also in Walter Blair, *Native American Humor* (San Francisco: Chandler Publishing Company, Inc., 1960), pp. 150-153; also in *Works: Tom Sawyer*, p. 4, p. 458 & p. 470, item 40.17.

[24] "The frontispiece [*Life and Sayings of Mrs. Partington*], a portrait of Mrs. Partington, engraved by Baker-Andrew, is unsigned and may also be after Coffin, although Mr. Howard Mott is the owner of what appears to be

the original drawing of this frontispiece and it is signed with the name of Wolcott. This frontispiece was used as a picture of Aunt Polly in the first edition of *The Adventures of Tom Sawyer*" (Hamilton, I, 93). Professor Mott regards Williams as the perpetrator in the Wolcott-Coffin-Williams confusion; "Since Williams was convivial, well read, and prankish, is it unreasonable to suppose that he fell behind in his work because of a spree and that in the emergency he, noticing the similarity between the two ladies, appropriated the picture of Ruth Partington by Wolcott and used it as a picture of Aunt Polly?" (Howard S. Mott, Jr., "The Origin of Aunt Polly, *Publisher's Weekly* [November 19, 1938], 1822).

[25]Hamilton, II, 152. The engraver's mark on all other Coffin cuts in the *Life and Sayings of Mrs. Partington* is N. Orr (Hamilton, I, 93). The engraver of the Coffin-Williams tail piece is Baker-Andrew.

[26]*MTLP*, p. 100, note 1.

[27]"In 1851-1852 the young Sam Clemens set type on some of B. P. Shillaber's sketches of Mrs. Partington . . . or at least he had a chance to read these sketches in its [Hannibal *Journal*] columns. Later, one of his first published works, 'The Dandy Frightening the Squatter,' appeared in Shillaber's *Carpet-Bag* in May 1852. [The Wolcott print of Mrs. Partington had appeared in No. 13 the year before.] And still later, as Mark Twain, the author mentioned Mrs. Partington in *Roughing It* (1872). So it is undoubtedly more than coincidence that Aunt Polly . . . turn[s] out to be extraordinarily like Mrs. Partington" (*Works: Tom Sawyer*, p. 4).

Clemens may also have given Williams another book, Dr. Calvin Cutter's *A Treatise on Anatomy, Physiology, and Hygiene*, which featured a white naked figure such as the one described in Chapter XX, to copy as a head piece, THE DISCOVERY, which appeared on p. 161 of the first edition.

[28]See *BMT*, pp. 29-30. The illustration, INJUN JOE'S TWO VIC-TIMS, appears on page 103 of the first edition.

[29]*Works: Tom Sawyer*, p. 521, item 79.5. The cut appears on page 70 of the first edition.

[30]*Works: Tom Sawyer*, p. 523, item 100.2. The cut appears on page 95 of the first edition. The sequence of cuts in the first edition does not follow exactly the manuscript cut sequence which did not include the head pieces or tail pieces (*Works: Tom Sawyer*, p. 508).

[31]SLC to EB, 5 November [1875], *MTLP*, p. 92. "Routledge had published authorized English editions of *The Innocents Abroad, (Burles-que) Autobiography, and First Romance, Roughing It*, and *The Gilded Age*. George Bentley, editor of *Temple Bar*, had been trying for several years to publish something by Mark Twain" (*Works: Tom Sawyer*, p. 18, note 32). *The Gilded Age* was the only illustrated English first edition.

[32]SLC to Moncure Conway, 5 January 1875, *MTinEng*, p. 67. See also *Works: Tom Sawyer*, p. 18, note. 33.

[33]M. D. Conway to Mrs. Conway, 18 January 1876, *MTinEng*, p. 69.

[34]Chatto and Windus to M. D. Conway, 31 January 1876, *MTinEng*, p. 71.

[35]Details on the various publishing ideas in *MTinEng*, p. 76-77.

[36]SLC to M. D. Conway, 9 April [1876], *MTLP*, p. 96. Conway received a five per cent commission as agent—an arrangement to which Clemens agreed (*MTinEng*, p. 76).

[37]*MTinEng*, p. 77.

[38]SLC to M. D. Conway, 9 April [1876], *MTLP*, p. 97. More on the size controversy in *Works: Tom Sawyer*, p. 19, and *MT&EB*, p. 113.

[39]Frank Bliss to SLC, 11 April 1876, *MT&EB*, p. 113. A week later Clemens had Bliss's cost estimates for pictures to be done at 25 cents per inch.

[40]*MTinEng*, p. 77.

[41]SLC to Howells, 18 January 1876, *MTHL*, I:121.

[42]SLC to M. D. Conway, 9 April 1876, *MTLP*, p. 96.

[43]SLC to Howells, 26 April [1876]. "Bliss made a failure in the matter of getting Tom Sawyer ready on time—the engravers assisting, as usual" (*MTHL*, I: 131-132).

[44]*MTinEng*, p. 78.

[45]"*BAL* 3367 . . . notes an 'Illustrated edition advertised in Ath [*Athenaeum*] Dec. 9, 1876,' a 'cheap edition, in illustrated boards' advertised in *Athenaeum*, 24 November 1877, and a 'new edition' with illustrations by True Williams, cloth, listed PC May 1, 1885. The first two items, which have not been located in the *Athenaeum* for those dates, were among the many printings of the first English edition, some of them misleadingly announced as new editions. Only the edition containing the Williams illustrations was a resetting and thus actually a new edition" (*Works: Tom Sawyer*, p. 503, note 1). "One illustration in the second English edition, signed 'Williams', was not in any specimen of the first American edition. . . . It was the tail piece for chapter 20 in the second English edition, captioned 'PURE ENJOYMENT.', and was an illustration of a boy eating what may have been supposed to be a fruit, a bun, or a piece of candy. The boy wears a cap with a visor and resembles none of the illustrations representing Tom Sawyer" (*Works: Tom Sawyer*, p. 509, note 6). See explanation for the caps, endnote 20 above.

[46]SLC to M. D. Conway, 2 November [1876], *MTLP*, pp. 105-106. In Norton, *Writing Tom Sawyer*, p. 88: "The English edition, first in terms of time, was followed closely by the pirated edition produced in Canada by Belford Brothers of Toronto. This printing of the novel appeared on or

about July 29, 1876, being copied from the English edition which had arrived there and had gone on sale a week earlier. . . . Evidence indicates the first knowledge of this happening came to him [Clemens] only several months later."

[47] *Works: Tom Sawyer*, p. 24.

[48] Donald Bruce McKeen, "Tom! You-U-U Tom! An Illustrated Study of Twain's Tom," 1969, unpublished, n. p. Hereafter cited as McKeen, "Tom." I am indebted to Prof. Tom Tenney for sending me this article on dress styles and illustration in *Tom Sawyer*.

[49] Mark Twain, *The Adventures of Tom Sawyer* (Hartford: The American Publishing Company, 1876), p. 36. Hereafter cited as *Tom Sawyer* (1876).

[50] McKeen, "Tom," n. p.

[51] *Tom Sawyer* (1876), p. 64.

[52] Mark Twain discusses whether to take Tom into manhood or leave him still a boy in *MT&EB*, p. 107; also in *Works: Tom Sawyer*, p. 13.

[53] *Tom Sawyer* (1876), p. 202.

[54] Warren Chappell, "Tom Sawyer and the Illustrators," *The Dolphin: A Periodical for all People Who Find Pleasure in Fine Books*, No. 4, Part 3 (New York: The Limited Editions Club, Spring 1941), 251. Hereafter cited as Chappell, *The Dolphin*.

[55] "True Williams, who illustrated the first American edition, shows the fence as being about four feet high, thus following the height Mark Twain originally wrote in the manuscript—and immediately canceled. A mild controversy over the nature of the fence [also] appears in Tyrus Hillway, 'Tom Sawyer's Fence,' *College English* 19, No. 4 (January 1958): 165-166, and Bruce R. McElderry, Jr., 'Tom Sawyer's Fence—Original Illustrations,' *College English* 19, No. 8 (May 1958): 370" (*Works: Tom Sawyer*, p. 471, item 46.12).

[56] Chappell, *The Dolphin*, 251.

[57] *MTCH*, pp. 71-72. Also in *MTCH* William Dean Howells, *Atlantic,* xxxvii (May 1876), 621-622; Moncure D. Conway [unsigned], London *Examiner* (17 June 1876), pp. 687-688; unsigned review, *Athenaeum* (24 June 1876), No. 2539, 851. In the Mark Twain Papers, Documents file, an unsigned review (Conway as author since it is a replica of the London *Examiner* review) from Cincinnati *Commercial* (26 June 1876), 5; an unsigned review (probably also Conway's), London *Times* (28 August 1876), p. 4; and an English review in *Academy* IX (24 June 1876), 605, which correlated the "bad little boy" of *SkNO* with Tom in *Tom Sawyer*. The reviewer could not, however, have meant a visual correlation since he was reviewing the unillustrated English edition.

List of Illustrations: *Sketches, New & Old* and *Tom Sawyer*

Mark Twain and His Illustrators: Index